FOOT THERAPY
FOR COMMON DISEASES

Compiled by Ji Qingshan and Li Jie

 FOREIGN LANGUAGES PRESS

First Edition 2001
Second Edition 2009

ISBN 978-7-119-05998-3
© Foreign Languages Press, Beijing, China, 2009
Published by Foreign Languages Press
24 Baiwanzhuang Road, Beijing 100037, China
http://www.flp.com.cn

Printed in the People's Republic of China

FOREWORD

Foot therapy is a branch of traditional Chinese medicine. It contains a number of unique therapeutic methods established and developed over a very long historical period of medical practice by many physicians of successive dynasties. Because the foot is closely linked with the internal organs through meridians, and fixed acupoints and corresponding areas of the internal organs are located on the foot, different stimuli applied to those acupoints and areas on foot can prevent and treat diseases, and improve and preserve health. Foot therapy methods are easy to learn and can cure many diseases, without any harmful side effects.

Employing the basic theories of traditional Chinese medicine and the modern medical knowledge and rich clinical experience of the authors, this book was written for the enlightenment of foreign readers so that they might understand, learn, and use this wonderful traditional therapy of China.

CONTENTS

Chapter 5

Other Foot Therapies

Chapter 6

Treatment of Common Diseases

Chapter 1

INTRODUCTION TO FOOT THERAPY

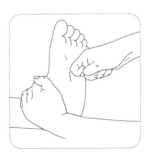

I. Origin and Development of Foot Therapy

Foot therapy applies different stimulations including massage, acupuncture, massage bar, and the local application of drugs to certain locations on the foot for the prevention and treatment of diseases and the preservation of health. This is accomplished by adjusting the functions of internal organs and promoting the circulation of qi and blood through the meridians.

As recorded in the history of Chinese medicine, foot therapy originated much earlier than other therapies. The ancients found that the pain and discomfort caused by external trauma or disease could be relieved by randomly or purposely applying some stimulation to certain areas of the foot with their hands or some instrument; and that fatigue could be relieved by washing the feet with hot water. They eventually discovered many useful methods of foot therapy, and following their investigations over a long historical period, modern foot massage, foot acupuncture, and the local application of drugs and foot baths were gradually established as independent therapies.

Ancient Chinese physicians began to treat diseases with foot massage about 2,000 years ago, and mention of foot therapy can be found in many medical books of the Jin, Ming and Qing dynasties. It spread to Japan during the Tang Dynasty and to European and American countries in the late Qing Dynasty. Now, foot therapy has been widely adopted and steadily developed through study and research done by more and more medical workers.

II. Foot Therapy Indications

Foot therapy is a safe, simple, effective and cheap treatment easy to learn and effective for the preservation of health and prevention and treatment of many diseases.

1. Indications

(1) Common diseases that can be quickly and effectively treated: Acute tonsillitis, toothache, headache, food poisoning, acute enteritis, dysentery, prostatitis, incontinence of urine, hemorrhoids, hiccups, neurotic stomachache, acute mastitis, acute otitis media, prolonged discharge of lochia after labor, Meniere's syndrome, stiff neck, periarthritis of shoulder, tennis elbow, knee joint injuries, intercostal neuralgia, acute wrist sprain, muscular strain of waist and foot pain.

(2) Chronic diseases requiring a longer course of therapy; Chronic bronchitis, hypertrophy of prostate gland, rheumatoid arthritis, hypertension, psychoneurosis, diabetes mellitus, coronary heart disease, arrhythmia of heart, hyperosteogeny, neuralgia sciatica, chronic superficial gastritis, chronic appendicitis, intestinal spasms, chronic colitis, habitual constipation, chronic cholecystitis, chronic nephritis, hypertrophy of lobules of mammary gland, dysmenorrhia and cervicitis.

(3) Stubborn diseases treatable with some therapeutic effect: Endometriosis, breast tumor, central retinitis, double vision, trigeminal neuralgia, liver cirrhosis with ascites, myoma of uterus, sexual intercourse pain, and atrophic gastritis.

2. Effects of foot therapy

(1) Relief of pain.

(2) Adjustment of the nervous system.

(3) Improvement of digestion and absorption by the digestive system.

(4) Adjustment of the balance of the neurohumoral system and improvement of adrenal cortex function.

(5) Improvement of immunity and body resistance, strengthening of physique, and improving resistance to the aging process.

3. Contraindications

Foot therapy is prohibited for patients with high fever (especially of unknown etiology), phlebitis or venous thrombosis of legs, diseases requiring surgery, gangrene, infection and pyogenic lesions of foot, suspicious bone fracture, extreme old age, extremely weak physique, and poor tolerance to treatment.

Chapter 2
FOOT DIAGNOSIS

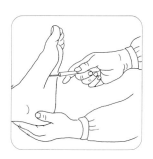

I. Reflecting Areas of Internal Organs on Foot

All major organs of the body have their corresponding projected areas on the foot. Their locations are regularly arranged and therefore easily remembered.

When the feet are put side by side, the reflecting areas of all the organs are arranged as a miniature human body in a sitting posture, with the trunk inclined forward and the legs crossed. The big toe corresponds to the head with its cerebrum, cerebellum and pituitary gland, and the proximal end of the big toe corresponds to the neck. The sense organs are arranged on the other toes. The arches of both feet, when placed side by side, correspond to the spinal column with the thoracic, lumbar, sacral and coccygeal segments arranged from the distal end to the proximal end of the arches. The anterior part of sole corresponds to the chest cavity, containing the heart and lungs; the middle part of the sole corresponds to the upper abdomen, including the liver, gallbladder, spleen, stomach, pancreas and kidneys; the posterior part of the sole corresponds to the lower abdomen, including the small intestine, colon, urinary bladder and genital organs; and the shoulder, elbow and knee joints are arranged along the lateral border of the foot from the anterior end to the posterior end, in sequence.

The reflecting areas of organs on the left side of the body are arranged on the left foot, and those on the right side are arranged on the right foot. Organs in pairs such as kidneys, lungs and ureters have their reflecting areas on both feet; and the organs lying on the body's midline, such as the cerebrum, cerebellum, nose, tonsils, stomach and spinal column have their projecting areas arranged along the medial borders of both feet. The projected areas of the liver, spleen, and ears are arranged along the lateral borders of both feet, but the projected areas of the cerebrum, frontal sinus, trigeminal nerves, eyes and ears are arranged on the contralateral foot, just as their nerves, which originate from both cerebral hemispheres,

6

are mutually crossed in the brain or spinal cord. Therefore, the projected area of the trigeminal nerve on the left foot is used to treat trigeminal neuralgia on the right of the face, and vice versa.

1. Diagram of Reflecting Areas on Right Sole:

1: head (brain), left hemisphere 2: left frontal sinus 3: brain stem and cerebellum 4: pituitary gland 5: left trigeminal nerve 6: nose 7: neck 8: left eye 9: left ear 11: trapezius muscle (neck, shoulder) 12: thyroid gland 13: parathyroid gland 14: lung and bronchus 15: stomach 16: duodenum 17: pancreas 18: liver 19: gallbladder 20: celiac plexus 21: adrenal gland 22: kidney 23: ureter 24: urinary bladder 26: cecum (appendix) 27: iliocecal valve 28: ascending colon 29: transverse colon 36: reproductive gland (ovary or testis)

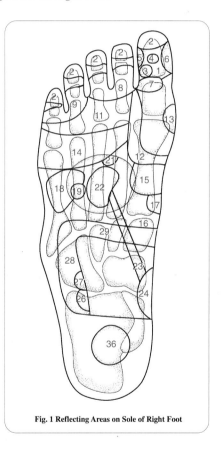

Fig. 1 Reflecting Areas on Sole of Right Foot

7

2. Diagram of Reflecting Areas on Left Sole:

1: head (brain), right hemisphere 2: right frontal sinus 3: brain stem and cerebellum 4: pituitary gland 5: right trigeminal nerve 6: nose 7: neck 8: right eye 9: right ear 11: trapezius muscle (neck, shoulder) 12: thyroid gland 13: parathyroid gland 14: lung, bronchus 15: stomach 16: duodenum 17: pancreas 20: celiac plexus 21: adrenal gland

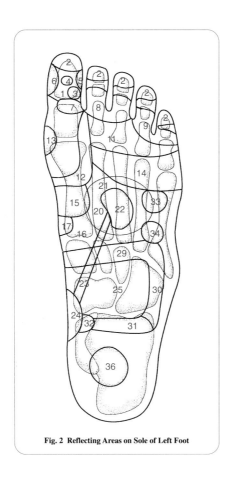

Fig. 2 Reflecting Areas on Sole of Left Foot

22: kidney 23: ureter 24: urinary bladder 25: small intestine 29: transverse colon 30: descending colon 31: rectum 32: anus 33: heart 34: spleen 36: reproductive gland (ovary or testis)

3. Diagram of Reflecting Areas on Lateral Side of Foot:

10: shoulder 35: knee 36: reproductive gland 37: lower abdomen 38: hip joint 39: lymph nodes (upper body) 42: balance organ (labyrinth) 43: chest 44: diaphragm 58: sciatic nerve 59: scapula 60: elbow joint 61: ribs

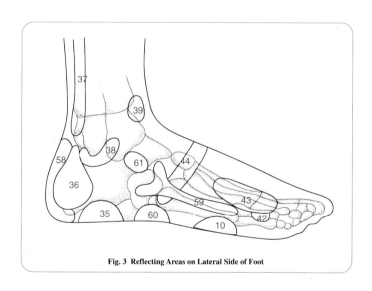

Fig. 3 Reflecting Areas on Lateral Side of Foot

4. Diagram of Reflecting Areas on Medial Side of Foot:

6: nose 13: parathyroid gland 24: urinary bladder 38: hip joint 40: lymph nodes (abdomen) 49: inguinal groove 50: uterus, prostate gland 51: penis, vagina, urethra 52: anus, rectum (hemorrhoid) 53: cervical spine 54: thoracic spine 55: lumbar spine 56: sacrum 57: coccyx 61: ribs

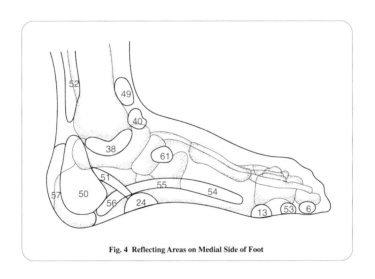

Fig. 4 Reflecting Areas on Medial Side of Foot

5. Diagram of Reflecting Areas on Dorsal Side of Foot:

39: lymph nodes (upper body) 40: lymph nodes (abdomen) 41: lymph nodes (chest) 42: balance organ (labyrinth) 43: chest 44: diaphragm 45: tonsils 46: lower jaw 47: palate 48: larynx, trachea, vocal cords 49: inguinal groove 61: ribs

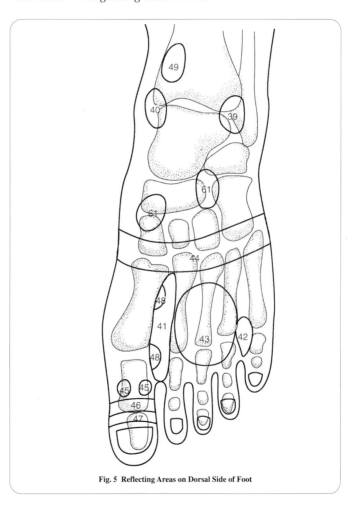

Fig. 5 Reflecting Areas on Dorsal Side of Foot

II. General Examination

For the proper diagnosis of diseases, the mental condition, facial complexion, physical constitution, sense organs and tongue coating all should be carefully examined. Through clinical practice over a long period of time, traditional Chinese physicians have found a close relationship between manifestations on the body surface and the functioning of the internal organs. Therefore, the examination of the appearance of body's surface is very useful for understanding pathological changes in the human body. However, external appearances are only superficial manifestations of disease and cannot show all its pathological properties. Therefore, a disease can be correctly diagnosed only after combining a general examination with other essential diagnostic techniques.

The feet should be carefully monitored for deformity, papule, changes in skin color, varicose veins, corns, tinea pedis or calluses which could indicate the presence of pathological changes in other parts of the body.

1. Examination of Skin:

Generally, the skin of the foot is rougher than the skin at any other part of the body. Abnormalities found on the skin of the foot may reflect pathological changes in the correspondent organs.

Examination may reveal the following lesions: Corns, rhagus, tinea pedis, plantar wart, wound, blister, burn lesion, venous aneurysm, nodule, papule, pigmentation, depression, desquamation, congestion, callus, edema, pustule, ulcer, keratinization, scar, flushing skin, or exudation as well as deformity and discoloration of the toe nails. The normal nail is smooth, shiny, hard and arc shaped. In a normal nail, the red color beneath it will fade away when pressure is applied to the nail, but will immediately be restored. Abnormal changes in the nails can be evidence of pathological changes occurring in the body. For example, an extremely downward curving nail may indicate the presence of a malignant tumor in the body; an inwardly curving nail may indicate alcoholism; a flat nail which fails to regain its color underneath after pressure is relieved and with a reduced semilunar area may indicate the presence of heart diseases; vertical creases may appear on the nails in people who are overfatigued from an irregular lifestyle or in patients with nervous system and respiratory symptoms; and horizontal creases may appear either before or after a critical disease.

The semilunar area of the nail can also indicate the body's general health. The height of this area in normal people is equal to one fifth the length of the nail. In patients with heart disease and hypertension, the semilunar area is greater than one fifth, and in patients with anemia, the height is much less than one fifth the length of the nail.

2.Examination of Tissue:

Because the foot is closely related to the entire body, the foot tissue may also reflect diseases of the internal organs. For example, edema and blood congestion usually appear in the ankle and Achilles tendon region, where the correspondent areas of internal organs in the chest and pelvic cavities are.

The Edema of the ankle region usually appears in patients with diseases of the kidney, heart or circulatory system, or in patients with blood congestion in the pelvic cavity due to disturbance of the veins, arteries, or lymphatic vessels, or of the nervous or endocrinal systems. Some small fatty polyps also may be found on both dorsums of the feet near the roots of the toes.

3.Examination of Bones:

Abnormal bones in the foot may produce general discomfort of the body.

A flat foot may affect the reflecting areas of the shoulder, spinal column and circulatory system; a right flat foot may affect the reflecting areas of the gallbladder and biliary tract, and a left flat foot may affect the reflecting area of the heart.

The talipes valgus may affect the reflecting areas of the thyroid gland and the cervical.

A deformity of big toe or other toes may affect the reflecting areas of the head and teeth.

Abnormal shape and tissue of the nails with fungal infection may affect the reflecting area of the head.

Sprain or congestion of the ankle joint may affect the reflecting areas of the pelvic cavity and hip joint.

III. Physical Examination of Foot

The physical examination of the foot can be divided into examination methods for the entire foot and examination methods for only one system. Examination of the entire foot is used to detect all reflecting areas on the foot one by one to discover pathological lesions in correspondent organs. This exam takes about one hour. The examination of one system is used to detect reflecting areas of only the diseased system. This exam takes only 10 minutes.

The methods of examination are as follows:

1. First, the patient is placed in a sitting posture on a stool, or in a supine lying posture on an examination table with the feet placed on the knees of the examiner, soles forward, or on a stool of similar height.

2. The foot of the patient is held by the examiner's left hand. An examination probe (Fig. 6) with a small bead of 2 mm diameter on

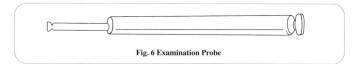

Fig. 6 Examination Probe

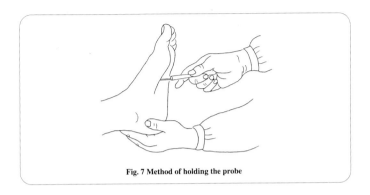

Fig. 7 Method of holding the probe

one end for pressing the reflecting areas of the foot, and with a handle of 4 mm diameter is held in the examiner's right hand. (Fig. 7).

3. The tip of the probe is pressed perpendicularly at the reflecting areas (Fig. 8). A pricking pain produced by the examination indicates a disease present in the correspondent organ. Otherwise, the organ is normal. If the disease is very serious, the pain may be too

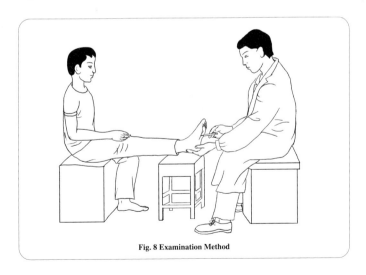

Fig. 8 Examination Method

severe to tolerate, and the examination of this area should be stopped immediately.

The pressure may vary from 0.5 to 1.0 kg according to the thickness of the muscles in different reflecting areas. It should be steadily applied and gradually increased to reach the deep layer of tissues before reaching the periosteum, because a false positive result may be produced due to hypersensitivity of the periosteum during stimulation.

The number of detecting spots in each reflecting area varies according to the size of the area. The detection may be applied to as many as 10 spots in a large area, or as few as 3-4 spots in a small area. A sharp pricking pain is the only indicator of a positive result, and a dull pain, numbness, distension or soreness cannot be taken as a diagnostic criterion. An area with even one positively detected spot can be selected as a therapeutic location.

4. Positive results of an examination of both feet should be recorded on the patient's medical chart and evaluated along with the findings of other diagnostic methods to make a correct diagnosis and an adequate therapeutic plan.

5. Several precautions must be taken, although this is a simple and reliable diagnostic method.

(1) Before examination, the criterion for a positive result should be clearly explained to the patient, who should be asked to give a correct answer, namely only a sharp pricking pain indicates a positive result.

(2) During examination the probe should be correctly held in the right hand and pressure applied adequately. The patient's foot should be held tightly with the left hand, the examined areas should be fully exposed, and the pressure should be applied steadily to a fixed spot.

(3) Detection in each reflecting area should be repeated 2-3 times

with the same pressure. At the same time, the patient's response to painful stimulation such as twitching and swinging the foot or a pained facial expression should be carefully monitored.

(4) Inquiry into the patient's medical history and the examination can be carried out simultaneously. For example, when the reflecting area of the thyroid gland (12) is examined, the examiner may also ask the symptoms suffered by patients with hyperthyroidism, including pathological leanness, fatigue, restlessness, hyperirritability, and profuse sweating. The physical signs of hyperthyroidism, including local mass, adhesion, and tenderness may also be examined to make a diagnosis of hyperthyroidism.

(5) If the result of this examination is doubtful, the patient may be asked to undergo some specific examinations with advanced instruments such as X-ray, CT scan and B-ultrasound to make a correct diagnosis and decide the proper foot therapy.

(6) The physical examination should be repeated once more after a course of foot therapy to check the therapeutic results and the patient's reactions. If the pricking pain in the reflecting area is still present and unchanged, another course of treatment should be applied again with the reflecting areas appropriately adjusted to improve the therapeutic effect.

(7) For diseases already diagnosed accurately, only the correlated reflecting areas should be detected to find positive areas for treatment. For example, in patients with colitis, only the reflecting areas of the digestive system should be examined, including the stomach 15, duodenum 16, pancreas 17, liver 18, gallbladder 19, small intestine 25, cecum and appendix 26, iliocecal valve 27, ascending colon 28, transverse colon 29, descending colon 30, rectum 31 and anus 32. Besides these reflecting areas, other positive areas can also be selected for treatment.

Chapter 3

FOOT MERIDIANS AND ACUPOINTS

I. Foot Meridians

The foot has three foot Yin (Taiyin spleen, Shaoyin kidney and Jueyin liver) meridians and three foot Yang (Yangming stomach, Taiyang urinary bladder and Shaoyang gallbladder) meridians passing through and including their origin and terminal points. The five Shu (well, spring, stream, river and sea) acupoints are also located on the foot. They are used to treat diseases of the head, face, sense organs, internal organs and trunk, and to adjust the functions of the whole body.

II. Foot Acupoints

1. Acupoints of the foot Yangming stomach meridian (Fig. 9):
(1) Jiexi (ST 41):
Location: At the junction of the leg and dorsum of foot, in a depression at the midpoint of the ankle joint and between the tendons of

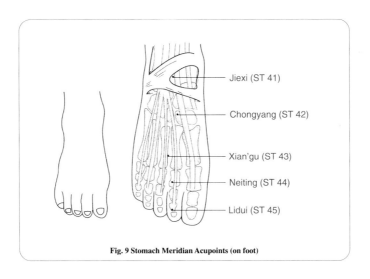

Jiexi (ST 41)

Chongyang (ST 42)

Xian'gu (ST 43)

Neiting (ST 44)

Lidui (ST 45)

Fig. 9 Stomach Meridian Acupoints (on foot)

the long extensor muscle of big toe and long extensor muscle of other toes.

Indications: Headache, vertigo, psychosis, abdominal distension, constipation, and paralysis of lower limb.

Application: The needle is vertically inserted for 1.6-3.3 cm.

(2) Chongyang (ST 42):

Location: On the dome of foot arch with the dorsal artery pulse of foot and between the tendons of long extensor muscle of big toe and long extensor muscle of other toes.

Indications: Deviation of mouth and eye, facial swelling, toothache, psychosis, epilepsy, stomachache and weakness of foot.

Application: The needle is vertically inserted for 1-1.6 cm and away from the artery.

(3) Xian'gu(ST 43):

Location: On the dorsum of foot and in a depression anterior to the junction of 2nd and 3rd metatarsal bones.

Indications: Edema of face and body, redness, swelling and pain of eyes, abdominal pain with gurgling sound, febrile diseases, and swelling and pain of dorsum of foot.

Application: The needle is vertically or obliquely inserted for 1.6-3.3 cm.

(4) Neiting (ST 44):

Location: On the dorsum of foot, between the 2nd and 3rd toes and on the dorsoplantar boundary of the web fold.

Indications: Toothache, sore throat, deviation of mouth, nasal bleeding, stomachache, regurgitation of sour fluid, abdominal distension, diarrhea, dysentery, constipation, febrile diseases, and swelling and pain of dorsum of foot.

Application: The needle is vertically or obliquely inserted for 1.6-2.6 cm.

(5) Lidui (ST 45):

Location: This is 0.3 cm from the lateral corner of nail of 2nd toe.

Indications: Nasal bleeding, toothache, sore throat, abdominal

distension, febrile diseases, dreaminess and psychosis.
Application: The needle is shallowly inserted for 0.3 cm.

2. Acupoints of the foot Taiyang urinary bladder meridian (Fig. 10):

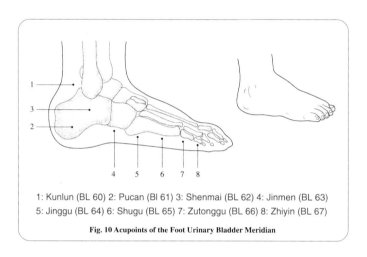

1: Kunlun (BL 60) 2: Pucan (Bl 61) 3: Shenmai (BL 62) 4: Jinmen (BL 63)
5: Jinggu (BL 64) 6: Shugu (BL 65) 7: Zutonggu (BL 66) 8: Zhiyin (BL 67)

Fig. 10 Acupoints of the Foot Urinary Bladder Meridian

(1) Kunlun (BL 60):
Location: Behind the lateral malleolus and in a depression between the tip of lateral malleolus and Achilles tendon.
Indications: Headache, stiff neck, vertigo, nasal bleeding, epilepsy, difficult labor, pain of lumbar and sacral region, and swelling and pain of heel.
Application: The needle is vertically inserted for 1.6-2.6 cm.
(2) Pucan (BL 61):
Location: On the lateral side of foot, behind and below lateral malleolus, directly below Kunlun and on the dorsoplantar boundary lateral to heel.
Indications: Paralysis of lower limb, heel pain, and epilepsy.

Application: The needle is vertically inserted for 1-1.6 cm.

(3) Shenmai (BL 62):

Location: On the lateral side of foot and in a depression directly below the lateral malleolus.

Indications: Headache, vertigo, psychosis, soreness and pain of waist and leg, eye redness and pain, and insomnia.

Application: The needle is vertically inserted for 1-1.6 cm.

(4) Jinmen (BL 63):

Location: On the lateral side of foot, directly below the anterior border of lateral malleolus and on the lower border of cuboid bone.

Indications: Headache, epilepsy, convulsions in children, lumbago, paralysis of lower limb, and pain of lateral malleolus.

Application: The needle is vertically inserted for 1-1.6 cm.

(5) Jinggu (BL 64):

Location: On the lateral side of foot, below the tuberosity of 5th metatarsal bone and on the dorsoplantar boundary.

Indications: Headache, stiff neck, milky eye, epilepsy, and lumbago.

Application: The needle is vertically inserted for 1-1.6 cm.

(6) Shugu (BL 65):

Location: On the lateral side of foot, behind the 5th metatarsophalangeal joint and on the dorsoplantar boundary.

Indications: Headache, stiff neck, vertigo, psychosis, and pain in waist and leg.

Application: The needle is vertically inserted for 1-1.6 cm.

(7) Zutonggu (BL 66):

Location: On the lateral side of foot, anterior to the 5th metatarsophalangeal joint and on the dorsoplantar boundary.

Indications: Headache, stiff neck, vertigo, nasal bleeding, and psychosis.

Application: The needle is vertically inserted for 0.6-1 cm.

(8) Zhiyin (BL 67):

Location: On the distal segment of little toe and 0.3 cm from the lateral corner of nail.

Indications: Headache, eye pain, nasal obstruction, nasal bleeding, abnormal fetal position, and difficult labor.
Application: The needle is shallowly inserted for 0.3 cm and moxibustion is applied for abnormal fetal position.

3. Acupoints of foot Shaoyang gallbladder meridian (Fig. 11):

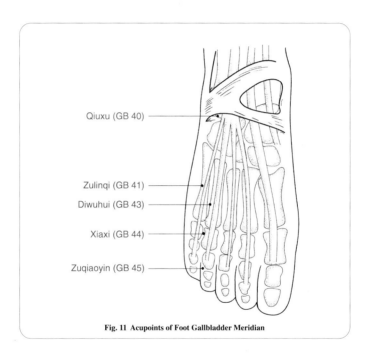

Qiuxu (GB 40)

Zulinqi (GB 41)
Diwuhui (GB 43)

Xiaxi (GB 44)

Zuqiaoyin (GB 45)

Fig. 11 Acupoints of Foot Gallbladder Meridian

(1) Qiuxu (GB 40):
Location: Below and anterior to the lateral malleolus and in a depression lateral to the tendon of long extensor muscle of toes.
Indications: Distension and pain in chest and flank, paralysis of lower limb, and malaria.
Application: The needle is vertically inserted for 1.6-2.6 cm.

(2) Zulinqi (GB 41):

Location: On the lateral side of dorsum of foot, behind the 4th metatarsophalangeal joint and in a depression lateral to the tendon of extensor muscle of little toe.

Indications: Redness, swelling and pain of eye, pain in flank and costal region, irregular menstruation, incontinence of urine, mastitis, tuberculosis of cervical lymph nodes, malaria, and instep pain.

Application: The needle is vertically inserted for 1-1.6 cm.

(3) Diwuhui (GB 42):

Location: On the lateral side of dorsum of foot, behind the 4th metatarsophylangeal joint, between the 4th and 5th metatarsal bones and on the medial border of tendon of extensor muscle of little toe.

Indications: Headache, red eyes, tinnitus, pain in flank, mastitis, hemoptysis due to internal injury and swelling and pain of dorsum of foot.

Application: The needle is vertically inserted for 1-1.6 cm.

(4) Xiaxi (GB 43):

Location: On the lateral side of dorsum of foot, between the 4th and 5th toes and on the dorsoplantar boundary of web fold.

Indications: Headache, vertigo, tinnitus, deafness, redness, swelling and pain of eye, pain in flank and costal region, febrile diseases, and mastitis.

Application: The needle is vertically inserted for 1-1.6 cm.

(5) Zuqiaoyin (GB 44):

Location: On the lateral side of 4th toe and 0.3 cm from the lateral corner of nail.

Indications: Headache, redness, swelling and pain of eye, deafness, sore throat, febrile diseases, insomnia, pain in flank, cough, and irregular menstruation.

Application: The needle is shallowly inserted for 0.3 cm or the bleeding therapy is applied.

4. Acupoints of foot Taiyin spleen meridian (Fig. 12):

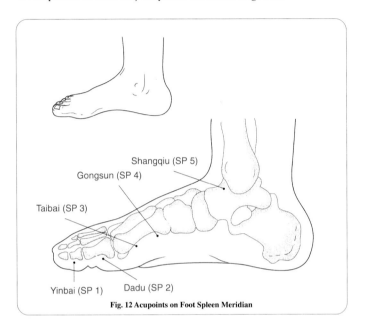

Shangqiu (SP 5)
Gongsun (SP 4)
Taibai (SP 3)
Yinbai (SP 1) Dadu (SP 2)

Fig. 12 Acupoints on Foot Spleen Meridian

(1) Yinbai (SP 1):
Location: On the medial side of distal segment of big toe and 0.3 cm from the medial comer of nail.

Indications: Abdominal distension, blood in stool, blood in urine, profuse menstrual discharge, profuse bloody uterine, psychosis, dreaminess, and convulsion.

Application: The needle is shallowly inserted for 0.3 cm.

(2) Dadu (SP 2):
Location: On the medial side of foot, in a depression below and anterior to the first metatarsophalangeal joint and on the dorsoplantar boundary.

Indications: Abdominal distension, stomachache, vomiting, diarrhea, constipation, and febrile diseases.

26

Application: The needle is vertically inserted for 1-1.6 cm.

(3) Taibai (SP 3):

Location: On the medial side of foot, in a depression below and posterior to the first metatarsophalangeal joint and on the dorsoplantar boundary.

Indications: Stomachache, abdominal distension and gurgling sound, diarrhea, constipation, hemorrhoid, and beriberi.

Application: The needle is vertically inserted for 1.6-2.6 cm.

(4) Gongsun (SP 4):

Location: On the medial side of foot and below and anterior to the base of first metatarsal bone.

Indications: Stomachache, vomiting, abdominal pain, diarrhea, and dysentery.

Application: The needle is vertically inserted for 2-4 cm.

(5) Shangqiu (SP 5):

Location: In a depression below and anterior to the medial malleolus and at the midpoint between the tubercle of navicular bone and tip of medial malleolus.

Indications: Abdominal distension, diarrhea, constipation, jaundice, and pain in ankle joint and foot.

Application: The needle is vertically inserted for 1.6-2.6 cm.

5. Acupoints of foot Jueyin liver meridian (Fig. 13):

(1) Dadun (LR 1):

Location: On the lateral side of distal segment of big toe and 0.3 cm from the lateral corner of nail.

Indications: Hernia, incontinence of urine, amenorrhea, profuse bloody uterine, prolapse of uterus, and epilepsy.

Application: The needle is obliquely inserted for 0.3-0.6 cm or the bleeding therapy is applied.

(2) Xingjian (LR 2):

Location: On the dorsal side of foot, between the first and 2nd toes and on the dorsoplantar boundary of web fold.

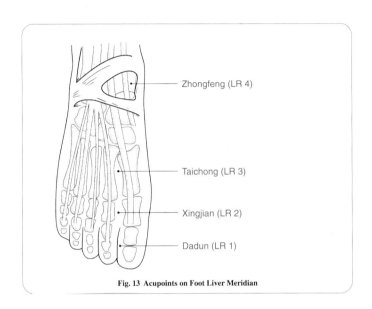

Fig. 13 Acupoints on Foot Liver Meridian

Labels in figure:
Zhongfeng (LR 4)
Taichong (LR 3)
Xingjian (LR 2)
Dadun (LR 1)

Indications: Headache, vertigo, redness, swelling and pain of eye, glaucoma, deviation of mouth, pain in flank, hernia, difficult urination, profuse bloody uterine, epilepsy, irregular menstruation, dysmenorrhea, leukorrhagia, and apoplexy.

Application: The needle is obliquely inserted for 1.6-2.6 cm.

(3) Taichong (LR 3):

Location: On the dorsal side of foot and in a depression in the first intermetatarsal space.

Indications: Headache, vertigo, redness, swelling and pain of eye, deviation of mouth, pain in flank, incontinence of urine, hernia, profuse bloody uterine, irregular menstruation, epilepsy, vomiting, convulsions in children, and paralysis of lower limb.

Application: The needle is vertically inserted for 1.6-2.6 cm.

6. Acupoints of foot kidney meridian (Fig. 14):

(1) Yongquan (KI 1):

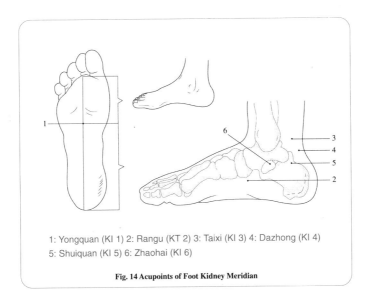

1: Yongquan (KI 1) 2: Rangu (KT 2) 3: Taixi (KI 3) 4: Dazhong (KI 4)
5: Shuiquan (KI 5) 6: Zhaohai (KI 6)

Fig. 14 Acupoints of Foot Kidney Meridian

Location: On the sole, at the junction of anterior one third and posterior two thirds of a line between the junction of 2nd and 3rd toes and heel and in the depression formed while flexing the instep.

Indications: Headache, dizziness, insomnia, vertigo, sore throat, aphonia, constipation, difficult urination, convulsions in children, psychosis, and syncope.

Application: The needle is vertically inserted for 1.6-3.3 cm.

(2) Rangu (KI 2):

Location: On the medial side of foot, below the tuberosity of navicular bone and on the dorsoplantar boundary.

Indications: Irregular menstruation, leukorrhagia, emission of semen, diabetes mellitus, diarrhea, hemoptysis, sore throat, difficult urination, tetanus in newborn babies and lockjaw.

Application: The needle is vertically inserted for 1.6-3.3 cm.

(3) Taixi (KI 3):

Location: On the medial side of foot, behind the medial malleolus and in a depression between the tip of medial malleolus and Achilles tendon.

Indications; Irregular menstruation, emission of semen, impotence, frequent urination, constipation, diabetes mellitus, hemoptysis, asthma, sore throat, toothache, insomnia, lumbago, deafness, and tinnitus.

Application: The needle is vertically inserted for 1.6-3.3 cm.

(4) Dazhong (KI 4):

Location: On the medial side of foot, below and behind the medial malleolus and in a depression medial to the attachment of Achilles tendon.

Indications: Retention of urine, incontinence of urine, constipation, hemoptysis, asthma, dementia, and heel pain.

Application: The needle is vertically inserted for 1-1.6 cm.

(5) Shuiquan (KI 5):

Location: On the medial side of foot, below and behind the medial malleolus, 3.3 cm below Taixi acupoint and in a depression medial to tuberosity of heelbone.

Indications: Irregular menstruation, dysmenorrhea, amenorrhea, prolapse of uterus, and difficult urination.

Application: The needle is vertically inserted for 1-1.6 cm.

(6) Zhaohai (KI 6):

Location: On the;medial side of foot and in a depression below the tip of medial malleolus.

Indications: Irregular menstruation, leukorrhagia, prolapse of uterus, frequent urination, retention of urine, constipation, dryness and pain in throat, epilepsy, and insomnia.

Application: The needle is vertically inserted for 1-1.6 cm.

III. Extra Foot Acupoints

Besides the regular meridianal acupoints, there are extra acupoints, discovered and accumulated through clinical practice by ancient physicians, which are also very useful and effective. The common extra acupoints on the foot are as follows (Figs. 15, 16, 17 and 18).

(1) Neihuai Qianxia (EX-F 1):

Location: One finger width anterior to the midpoint of lower border of medial malleolus (Fig. 15).

Indication: Regurgitation of food.

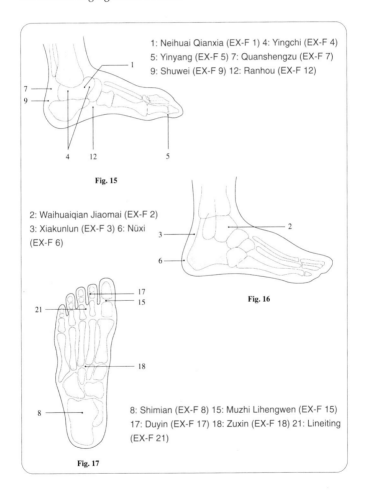

1: Neihuai Qianxia (EX-F 1) 4: Yingchi (EX-F 4)
5: Yinyang (EX-F 5) 7: Quanshengzu (EX-F 7)
9: Shuwei (EX-F 9) 12: Ranhou (EX-F 12)

Fig. 15

2: Waihuaiqian Jiaomai (EX-F 2)
3: Xiakunlun (EX-F 3) 6: Nüxi
(EX-F 6)

Fig. 16

8: Shimian (EX-F 8) 15: Muzhi Lihengwen (EX-F 15)
17: Duyin (EX-F 17) 18: Zuxin (EX-F 18) 21: Lineiting
(EX-F 21)

Fig. 17

(2) Waihuaiqian Jiaomai (EX-F 2):

Location: On the dorsal side of ankle joint and at the junction of medial three fourths and lateral one fourth of a connecting line between the tips of medial and lateral malleolus (Fig. 16).

Indication: Toothache.

(3) Xiakunlun (EX-F 3):

Location: On the anterior border of Achilles tendon and 3.3 cm below the tip of lateral malleolus (Fig. 16).

Indications: Bi-syndrome due to cold pathogen, lumbago, migraine, hemiplegia, and painful walking.

(4) Yingchi (EX-F 4):

Location: In the depressions anterior and posterior to the lower border of medial malleolus (Fig. 15),

Indications: Profuse menstrual discharge and discharge of red and white leukorrhea.

(5) Yinyang (EX-F 5):

Location: At the medial end of the interphalangeal crease of big toe (Fig. 15).

Indications: Syncope, discharge of red and white leukorrhea, and diarrhea.

(6) Nuxi (EX-F 6):

Location: At the midpoint of heel bone (Fig. 16).

Indications: Vomiting, diarrhea, muscular spasms, osteomyelitis of maxillary bone, gingivitis, convulsions, and mental diseases.

(7) Quanshengzu (EX-F 7):

Location: On the posterior midline of Achilles tendon and at the midpoint of the crease above heel bone (Fig. 15).

Indications: Difficult labor, lumbago, and spasm of esophagus.

(8) Shimian (EX-F 8):

Location: On the sole and at the crossing point of the midline of sole and the connecting line of medial and lateral malleolus (Fig. 17).

Indications: Insomnia and pain of the sole.

(9) Shuwei (EX-F 9):

Location: At the midpoint of upper border of heel bone (Fig. 15).

Indication: Tubercles of cervical lymph nodes.

(10) Quchi (EX-F 10):

Location: On the medial side of foot arch, below and anterior to medial malleolus and in a depression between the tendons of anterior tibial muscle and long extensor muscle of big toe (Fig. 18).

Indications: Pain in lower abdomen, emission of semen, and hernia.

(11) Tongli (EX-F 11):

Location: On the dorsum of foot and 1.6 cm anterior to the posterior end of tile interosseous space between 4th and 5th metatarsal bones (Fig. 18).

Indication: Profuse menstrual discharge.

(12) Ranhou (EX-F 12):

Location: This is 1.3 cm posterior to Rangu (KI 2) of kidney meridian (Fig. 15).

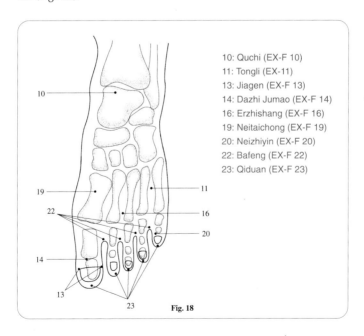

10: Quchi (EX-F 10)
11: Tongli (EX-11)
13: Jiagen (EX-F 13)
14: Dazhi Jumao (EX-F 14)
16: Erzhishang (EX-F 16)
19: Neitaichong (EX-F 19)
20: Neizhiyin (EX-F 20)
22: Bafeng (EX-F 22)
23: Qiduan (EX-F 23)

Fig. 18

Indication: Indigestion.

(13) Jiagen (EX-F 13):

Location: On the dorsal side of big toe and beside the medial and lateral comers of nail (Fig. 18).

Indication: Hernia.

(14) Dazhi Jumao (EX-F 14):

Location: On the dorsal side of big toe and in the hair on the interphalangeal joint of this toe (Fig. 18).

Indications: Apoplexy with coma, headache, vertigo, hernia, and orchitis.

(15) Muzhi Lihengwen (EX-F 15):

Location: On the plantar side of big toe and at the midpoint of crease of interphalangeal joint (Fig. 17).

Indication: Hernia.

(16) Erzhishang (EX-F 16):

Location: At the midpoint between Neiting (ST 44) and Xiangu (ST 43) (Fig. 18).

Indication: Edema.

(17) Duyin (EX-F 17):

Location: On the plantar side of foot and at the midpoint of the crease of 2nd metatarsophalangeal joint (Fig. 17).

Indications: Pregnancy vomiting, hematemesis, difficult labor, retention of dead fetus or placenta, hernia, and irregular menstruation.

(18) Zuxin (EX-F 18):

Location: At the midpoint of a connecting line between the tip of 2nd toe and the posterior border of heel (Fig. 17).

Indications: Profuse uterine bleeding, headache, vertigo, epilepsy, pain of the sole, and shock.

(19) Neitaichong (EX-F 19):

Location: On the dorsal side of foot, in a depression on the tibial side of tendon of long extensor muscle of big toe and on the opposite side of Taichong (LR 3) (Fig. 18).

Indications: Hernia with obstruction and dyspnea.

(20) Neizhiyin (EX-F 20):

Location: This is 0.3 cm from the medial comer of nail of little toe and opposite Zhiyin (BL 67) (Fig. 18).

Indications: Convulsions in children, syncope, and hysteria.

(21) Lineiting (EX-F 21):

Location: On the plantar side of foot, between the 2nd and 3rd toes and on the opposite side of Neiting (ST 44) (Fig. 17).

Indications: Convulsions in children, epilepsy, and pain in toes.

(22) Bafeng (EX-F 22):

Location: On the dorsum of foot, between all neighboring toes and on the dorsoplantar boundary of the web folds (Fig. 18).

Indications: Headache, toothache, poisonous snake bite, redness and swelling of instep, and irregular menstruation.

(23) Qiduan (EX-F 23):

Location: On the tips of all ten toes (Fig. 18).

Indications: Beriberi, paralysis of toes, redness and swelling of instep, and emergency treatment.

Chapter 4
FOOT ACUPUNCTURE

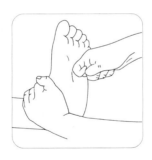

Foot acupuncture is applied to special acupoints on the foot (FA) other than the acupoints of the 14 meridians to treat diseases of the entire body. As a branch of traditional acupuncture, it is adopted according to the meridianal theories and on the basis of the close relationships between foot and meridians, internal organs, and qi and blood to treat diseases by stimulating the circulation of meridianal qi, adjusting the functions of internal organs, tissues, qi and blood, enriching vital energy, and expelling pathogens.

Foot acupuncture is a simple and effective therapy with numerous indications.

I. Method of Localizing Foot Acupoints

The correct localization of foot acupoints is very important for obtaining good therapeutic effects.

1. Proportional bone measurement (Figs. 19 and 20):

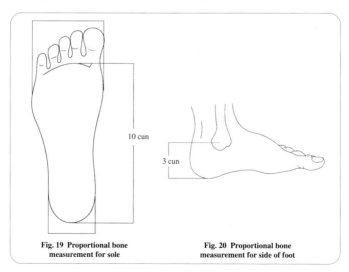

10 cun

3 cun

Fig. 19 Proportional bone measurement for sole

Fig. 20 Proportional bone measurement for side of foot

(1) The distance between the heel border and the root of 3rd toe is divided into 10 cun (one cun is about 3.3 cm).

(2) The distance from tip of medial of lateral malleolus to medial or lateral border of foot is divided into 3 cun.

(3) The distance between medial border (dorsoplantar boundary) of first metatarsophalangeal joint and lateral border (dorsoplantar boundary) of 5th metatarsophalangeal joint on both dorsal and plantar side is divided into 5 cun.

(4) The widest part of the heel is divided into 3 cun. These standards can be applied to all average-size adults of any age and either sex.

2. Surface anatomical landmarks:

The acupoints are located according to surface anatomical landmarks, including the creases of toes, tips of toes, metatarsophalangeal joints, capitula of metatarsal bones, terminals of creases between toes, tips of medial and lateral malleoli, and tuberosity of navacular bone. For example, the dysmenorrhea acupoint (FA-M 3) is 2 cun below the tip of medial malleolus; the bed-wetting acupoint (FA-P 21) is at the midpoint of the first crease of the little toe.

II. Foot Acupoints (FA)

According to the latest medical literature, there are a total of 39 foot acupoints, including 22 acupoints on the sole, 12 acupoints on dorsum of foot, 4 acupoints on medial side of foot and one acupoint on lateral side of foot.

1. Foot acupoints on the sole (Fig. 21):

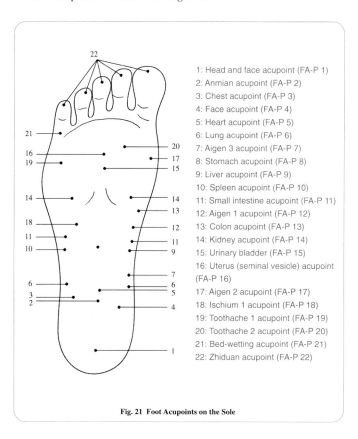

1: Head and face acupoint (FA-P 1)
2: Anmian acupoint (FA-P 2)
3: Chest acupoint (FA-P 3)
4: Face acupoint (FA-P 4)
5: Heart acupoint (FA-P 5)
6: Lung acupoint (FA-P 6)
7: Aigen 3 acupoint (FA-P 7)
8: Stomach acupoint (FA-P 8)
9: Liver acupoint (FA-P 9)
10: Spleen acupoint (FA-P 10)
11: Small intestine acupoint (FA-P 11)
12: Aigen 1 acupoint (FA-P 12)
13: Colon acupoint (FA-P 13)
14: Kidney acupoint (FA-P 14)
15: Urinary bladder (FA-P 15)
16: Uterus (seminal vesicle) acupoint (FA-P 16)
17: Aigen 2 acupoint (FA-P 17)
18: Ischium 1 acupoint (FA-P 18)
19: Toothache 1 acupoint (FA-P 19)
20: Toothache 2 acupoint (FA-P 20)
21: Bed-wetting acupoint (FA-P 21)
22: Zhiduan acupoint (FA-P 22)

Fig. 21 Foot Acupoints on the Sole

(1) Head and face acupoint (FA-P 1):

Location: On the midline and one cun (3.3 cm) from the posterior heel border.

Indications: Common cold, headache, maxillary sinusitis, and rhinitis.

Application: The needle is vertically inserted for 1-1.6 cm.

(2) Anmian acupoint (FA-P 2):

Location: On the midline, 3 cun (10 cm) from the posterior heel border and at the midpoint on the connecting line of medial and lateral malleoli.

Indications: Insomnia, psychosis, hysteria, neurasthenia, and hypotension.

Application: The needle is vertically inserted for 1-1.6 cm.

(3) Chest acupoint (FA-P 3):

Location: This is one cun (3.3 cm) lateral to the midline of foot, 3 cun (10 cm) from the posterior heel border and 1 cun lateral to Anmian acupoint.

Indications: Chest pain and distress, and intercostal neuralgia.

Application: The needle is vertically inserted for 1.6-2.6 cm.

(4) Face acupoint (FA-P 4):

Location: This is one cun (3.3 cm) medial to Anmian acupoint.

Indications: Trigeminal neuralgia, facial palsy, and facial itching.

(5) Heart acupoint (FA-P 5):

Location: On the midline and 3.5 cun (11.6 cm) from the posterior border of heel.

Indications: Hypertension, heart palpitations, heart pain, sore throat, stiff tongue, tongue pain, and insomnia.

Application: The needle is vertically inserted for 1-1.6 cm.

(6) Lung acupoint (FA-P 6):

Location: They are 1.5 cun (5 cm) on either side of heart acupoint

Indications: Cough, asthma, and chest pain.

Applicatioin: The needle is vertically inserted for 1-1.6 cm or obliquely inserted for 1.6-3.3 cm.

(7) Aigen 3 acupoint (FA-P 7):

Location: This is 1.5 cun (5 cm) medial to the midline of sole, 4 cun (13.3 cm) from posterior heel border and 0.5 cun (1.6 cm) medial to lung acupoint.

Indications: Relief of pain, spasms and other symptoms of cancers of nasopharynx, neck, lungs, and upper and middle segment of esophagus.

Application: The needle is vertically inserted for 1.6-2.6 cm or obliquely inserted toward medial malleolus or heel for 2.6-4 cm.

(8) Stomach acupoint (FA-P 8):

Location: On the midline of sole and 5 cun (16 cm) from the posterior heel border.

Indications: Diseases of stomach, vomiting, indigestion, and insomnia.

Application: The needle is vertically or obliquely inserted for 1.6-3.3 cm.

(9) Liver acupoint (FA-P 9):

Location: This is 2 cun (6.6 cm) medial to stomach acupoint.

Indications: Acute or chronic hepatitis, cholecystitis, intercostal neuralgia, and eye diseases.

Application: The needle is vertically or backward obliquely inserted for 1.6-3.3 cm.

(10) Spleen acupoint (FA-P 10):

Location: This is one cun (3.3 cm) lateral to stomach acupoint.

Indications: Indigestion, diarrhea, retention of urine, blood diseases, and insomnia.

Application: The needle is vertically or obliquely inserted to medial side for 1.6-3.3 cm.

(11) Small intestine acupoint (FA-P 11):

Location: They are 1.5 cun (5 cm) medial and lateral to the midline and 5.5 cun (18.3 cm) from posterior heel border.

Indications: Abdominal pain, diarrhea, intestinal gurgling, and dysentery.

Application: The needle is vertically or obliquely inserted for 2.6-4 cm.

(12) Aigen 1 acupoint (FA-P 12):

Location: It is 2 cun (6.6 cm) medial to the midline of sole and 6 cun (20 cm) from posterior heel border.

Indications: Relief of pain and symptoms of cancers of lower end of esophagus, stomach, and cardia.

Application: The needle is vertically inserted for 1-1.6 cm or pierced toward medioposterior side for 2.6-4 cm.

(13) Colon acupoint (FA-P 13):

Location: This is 2 cun (6.6 cm) medial to the midline of sole and 6.5 cun (21.6 cm) from posterior heel border.

Indications: Abdominal pain, vomiting, diarrhea, and dysentery.

Application: The needle is vertically inserted for 2.6-3.3 cm.

(14) Kidney acupoint (FA-P 14):

Location: They are 1.5 cun (5 cm) medial and lateral to Yongquan (KI 1).

Indications: Headache, vertigo, psychosis, retention of urine, incontinence of urine, and lumbago.

Application: The needle is vertically or obliquely inserted toward Yongquan for 2.6-4 cm.

(15) Urinary bladder acupoint (FA-P 15):

Location: On the midline of sole and 2 cun (6.6 cm) posterior to the root of 3rd toe.

Indications: Retention of urine, bed-wetting, and incontinence of urine.

Application: The needle is vertically or obliquely inserted for 2.6-4 cm.

(16) Uterus (seminal vesicle) acupoint (FA-P 16):

Location: On the midline of sole and 1.5 cun (5 cm) posterior to the root of 3rd toe.

Indications: Irregular menstruation, dysmenorrhea, leukorrhagia, retention of urine, and orchitis.

Application: The needle is vertically inserted for 1.6-2.6 cm.

(17) Aigen 2 acupoint (FA-P 17):

Location: This is 2.5 cun (8.3 cm) medial to urinary bladder acupoint.

Indications: Relief of pain and other symptoms of cancers in organs below umbilicus or metastatic tumors in lymph nodes.

Application: The needle is vertically or backward obliquely inserted for 2.6-4 cm.

(18) Ischium 1 acupoint (FA-P 18):

Location: This is 4 cun (13.3 cm) posterior to the root of 4th toe.

Indications: Neuralgia sciatica, lumbago, urticaria, and shoulder pain.

Application: The needle is vertically or backward obliquely inserted for 1.6-3.3 cm.

(19) Toothache 1 acupoint (FA-P 19):

Location: This is one cun (3.3 cm) posterior to the root of little toe.

Indication: Toothache.

Application: The needle is vertically or backward obliquely inserted for 1.6-3.3 cm.

(20) Toothache 2 acupoint (FA-P 20):

Location: This is one cun (3.3 cm) posterior to the junction of the big and 2nd toes.

Indication: Toothache.

Application: The needle is vertically inserted for 1.6-3.3 cm.

(21) Bed-wetting acupoint (FA-P 21):

Location: At the midpoint of the crease of first interphalangeal joint of little toe.

Indications: Bed-wetting and frequent urination.

Application: The needle is vertically or backward obliquely inserted for 1-1.6 cm.

(22) Zhiduan (tip of toes) acupoint (FA-P 22):

Location: They are at the tips of all ten toes and 0.3 cm from the edge of nail.

Indications: Apoplexy with coma, numbness of toes, gangrene of toes, and beriberi.

Application: The needle is shallowly inserted for 0.3-0.6 cm and the bleeding therapy may be applied to those acupoints with 3-edged needle.

2. Acupoints on dorsum of foot (Fig. 22):

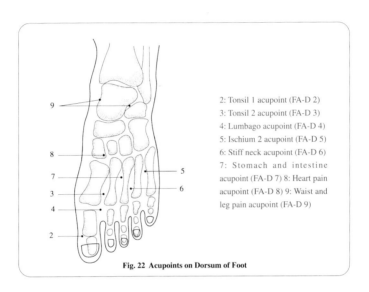

2: Tonsil 1 acupoint (FA-D 2)
3: Tonsil 2 acupoint (FA-D 3)
4: Lumbago acupoint (FA-D 4)
5: Ischium 2 acupoint (FA-D 5)
6: Stiff neck acupoint (FA-D 6)
7: Stomach and intestine acupoint (FA-D 7) 8: Heart pain acupoint (FA-D 8) 9: Waist and leg pain acupoint (FA-D 9)

Fig. 22 Acupoints on Dorsum of Foot

(1) Headache acupoint (FA-D 1):

Location: On the dorsum of foot and on the dorsoplantar boundary medial to the metatarsophalangeal joints of 2nd-4th toes.

Indication: Headache.

Application: The needle is shallowly inserted for 0.3-0.6 cm.

(2) Tonsil 1 acupoint (FA-D 2):

Location: On the big toe, at the metatarsophalangeal joint and medial to the tendon of long extensor muscle of the big toe.

Indications: Acute tonsillitis, epidemic parotitis, eczema, and urticaria.

Application: The needle is shallowly inserted for 0.6-1 cm.

(3) Tonsil 2 acupoint (FA-D 3):

Location: At the midpoint between Taichong (LR 3) and Xingjian (LR 2).

Indications: Acute tonsillitis and epidemic parotitis.

Application: The needle is vertically inserted for 1.6-2.6 cm.

(4) Lumbago acupoint (FA-D 4):

Location: In a depression lateral to the capitulum of first metatarsal bone.

Indications: Acute waist sprain and lumbago.

Application: The needle is vertically inserted for 1.6-2.6 cm.

(5) Ischium 2 acupoint (FA-D 5):

Location: On the dorsum of foot and at the midpoint and between Zulinqi (GB 41) and Diwuhui (GB 42).

Indication: Neuralgia sciatica.

Application: The needle is vertically inserted for 2-2.6 cm or obliquely inserted toward Ischium 1 acupoint (FA-P 18) for 3.3-5 cm.

(6) Stiff neck acupoint (FA-D 6):

Location: On the dorsum of foot and 2 cun (6.6 cm) behind the junction of 3rd and 4th toes.

Indication: Stiff neck.

Application: The needle is vertically inserted for 1.6-2.6 cm.

(7) Stomach and intestine acupoint (FA-D 7):

Location: On the dorsum of foot and 3 cun (10 cm) behind the junction of 2nd and 3rd toes.

Indications: Acute and chronic gastroenteritis and gastric and duodenal peptic ulcer.

Application: The needle is vertically or upward obliquely inserted for 3.3-5 cm.

(8) Heart pain acupoint (FA-D 8):

Location: This is 2.5 cun (8.3 cm) below Jiexi (ST 41).

Indications: Heart pain, heart palpitations, asthma, and common cold.

Application: The needle is vertically inserted for 1-1.6 cm.

(9) Waist and leg pain acupoint (FA-D 9):

Location: They are 0.5 cun (1.6 cm) below Jiexi (ST 41) and in bilateral depressions.

Indications: Lumbago, and pain and spasm of lower limb.

3. Acupoints on medial side of foot (Fig. 23):

(1) Vertigo acupoint (FA-M 1):

Location: On the medial side of foot and in a depression above tuberosity of navicular bone.

Indications: Vertigo, headache, hypertension, parotitis, and acute tonsillitis.

Application: The needle is vertically inserted for 1-1.6 cm.

(2) Dysmenorrhea 1 acupoint (FA-M 2):

Location: This is 2 cun (6.6 cm) directly below the tip of medial malleolus.

Indications: Functional uterine bleeding, irregular menstruation, and dysmenorrhea.

Application: The needle is vertically or obliquely inserted for 1.6-2.6 cm.

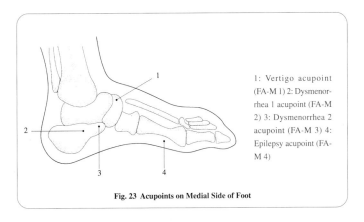

1: Vertigo acupoint (FA-M 1) 2: Dysmenorrhea 1 acupoint (FA-M 2) 3: Dysmenorrhea 2 acupoint (FA-M 3) 4: Epilepsy acupoint (FA-M 4)

Fig. 23 Acupoints on Medial Side of Foot

(3) Dysmenorrhea 2 acupoint (FA-M 3):

Location: On the medial side of foot and in a depression below and behind the tuberosity of navicular bone.

Indications: Dysmenorrhea, functional uterine bleeding, and adnexitis.

Application: The needle is vertically inserted for 2.6-3.3 cm.

(4) Epilepsy acupoint (FA-M 4):

Location: At the midpoint between Taibai (SP 3) and Gongsun (SP 4).

Indications: Epilepsy, hysteria, and neurasthenia.

Application: The needle is vertically inserted for 2.6-4 cm.

4. Acupoint on lateral side of foot (Fig. 24):

Buttocks acupoint (FA-L 1):

Location: This is one cun (3.3 cm) above Kunlun (BL 60).

Indications: Neuralgia sciatica, headache, and abdominal pain.

Application: The needle is vertically or obliquely inserted for 2.6-4 cm.

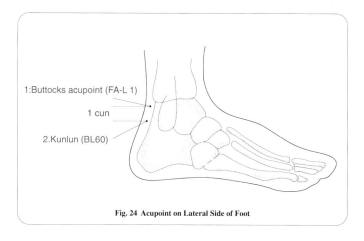

Fig. 24 Acupoint on Lateral Side of Foot

III. Principles for Selecting Acupoints

1. According to symptoms of diseases:
The effective acupoints of each important symptom of a disease may be used simultaneously. For example, the Headache acupoint (FA-D 1) is used to treat headaches and the Anmian acupoint (FA-P 2) is used to treat insomnia. Acupoints with similar functions can be used at the same time, for instance, the Ischium 1 acupoint (FA-P 18) and Ischium 2 acupoint (FA-D 5) can be used together to treat neuralgia sciatica. The acupoints for the symptoms of a disease, and those for the disease itself, may be used together to treat the patient. In this way, the Anmian and Headache acupoints may be used to treat patients suffering from insomnia and headache.

2. According to the location of lesions:
The Stomach acupoint (FA-P 8) may be used to treat stomachache and the Urinary bladder acupoint (FA-P 15) and Kidney acupoint (FA-P 14) may be used to treat retention of urine.

3. According to the theory of internal organs:
Besides the Vertigo acupoint (FA-M 1), the Liver acupoint (FA-P 9) and Kidney acupoint (FA-P 14) can also be used to treat vertigo due to deficiency of liver and kidney Yang and exacerbation of liver Yang. The liver acupoint can be used to treat eye diseases because the eyes are the external orifices of the liver; and the kidney acupoint can be used to treat ear diseases because the ears are the external orifices of the kidney.

IV. Application Methods

1. Posture of patient:
The patient is usually put in a supine lying posture with both legs

extended straight and both feet comfortably and stably placed for the physicians to conveniently locate the acupoint and apply acupuncture.

2. Sterilization:

The acupuncture instruments and the physician's hands should be routinely sterilized and the patient's skin should be locally sterilized with cottonballs of 75 percent alcohol.

3. Acupuncture techniques:

Acupuncture needles 3.3-6.6 cm long are inserted with the right hand into the acupoints, while the acupuncturist presses with the left hand. The needles are inserted vertically, obliquely, or horizontally to the proper depth according to the properties of the acupoints and clinical requirement. Generally, a twisting technique with moderate stimulation is applied to treat most diseases, but strong stimulation should be applied to treat psychosis and acute pain.

4. Retention of needle:

For common diseases, the needles may be removed after the needling sensation has been obtained or retained for 3-5 minutes. However, the needles may be retained for 20-30 minutes for certain diseases and repeatedly twisted at 5-10 minute intervals or stimulated by electric current.

5. Therapeutic course:

For common diseases, acupuncture is applied once a day or every other day, but it may be applied twice a day for acute diseases and severe pain. A therapeutic course consists of ten treatments.

V. Precautions

1. Because the needling sensation of foot acupuncture is very strong, the special characteristics of this therapy should be explained topatients before they receive treatment in order to assure their cooperation. For nervous or first-time patients, acupuncture should be applied gently with the needles quickly removed in order to avoid distress.

2. The foot should be carefully sterilized before applying acupuncture and the patient asked to keep the foot clean after treatment to prevent infection.

3. The needles should be carefully inserted and manipulated at the acupoints beside bones to avoid injuring the periosteum. The blood vessels should also be protected against injury.

Acupoints for Symptoms and Common Diseases

1. Headache: Head and face acupoint (FA-P 1), Kidney acupoint (FA-P 14), Headache acupoint (FA-D 1), Vertigo acupoint (FA-M 1) and Buttocks acupoint (FA-L 1).
2. Insomnia: Anmian acupoint (FA-P 2), Heart acupoint (FA-P 5), Stomach acupoint (FA-P 8), Spleen acupoint (FA-P 10) and Epilepsy acupoint (FA-M 4).
3. Vertigo: Kidney acupoint (FA-P 14), Vertigo acupoint (FA-M 1) and Liver acupoint (FA-P 9).
4. Apoplexy with coma: Zhiduan acupoint (FA-P 22).
5. Facial palsy: Face acupoint (FA-P 4), and Head and face acupoint (FA-P 1).
6. Trigeminal neuralgia: Face acupoint (FA-P 4), and Head and face acupoint (FA-P 1).
7. Tonsillitis: Heart acupoint (FA-P 5), Tonsil 1 acupoint (FA- D 2),

Tonsil 2 acupoint (FA-D 3) and Vertigo acupoint (FA-M 1).

8. Eye diseases: Liver acupoint (FA-P 9), and Head and face acupoint (FA-P 1).

9. Ear diseases: Kidney acupoint (FA-P14).

10. Rhinitis: Head and face acupoint (FA-P 1).

11. Toothache: Toothache 1 acupoint (FA-P 19) and Toothache 2 acupoint (FA-P 20).

12. Parotitis: Tonsil 1 acupoint (FA-D 2), Tonsil 2 acupoint (FA-D 3) and Vertigo acupoint (FA-M 1).

13. Hypertension: Heart acupoint (FA-P 5), Liver acupoint (FA-P 9), Kidney acupoint (FA-P 14) and Vertigo acupoint (FA-M 1).

14. Psychosis and hysteria: Anmian acupoint (FA-P 2), Kidney acupoint (FA-P 14) and Epilepsy acupoint (FA-M 4).

15. Epilepsy: Epilepsy acupoint (FA-M 4), Liver acupoint (FA-P 9), Kidney acupoint (FA-P 14) and Anmian acupoint (FA-P 2).

16. Retention of urine: Spleen acupoint (FA-P 10), Kidney acupoint (FA-P 14), Urinary bladder acupoint (FA-P 15) and Uterus acupoint (FA-P 16).

17. Bed-wetting: Urinary bladder acupoint (FA-P 15), Kidney acupoint (FA-P 14) and Bed-wetting acupoint (FA-P 21).

18. Dysmenorrhea: Uterus acupoint (FA-P 16), Dysmenorrhea 1 acupoint (FA-M 2) and Dysmenorrhea 2 acupoint (FA-M 3).

19. Stiff neck: Stiff neck acupoint (FA-D 6).

20. Stomachache: Stomach acupoint (FA-P 8), Stomach and intestine acupoint (FA-D 7) and Liver acupoint (FA-P 9).

21. Vomiting: Stomach acupoint (FA-P 8) and Colon acupoint (FA-P 13).

22. Abdominal pain: Small intestine acupoint (FA-P 11), Colon acupoint (FA-P 13), Stomach and intestine acupoint (FA-D 7) and Buttocks acupoint (FA-L 1).

23. Dysentery: Small intestine acupoint (FA-P 11), Colon acupoint (FA-P 13) and Stomach and intestine acupoint (FA-D 7).

24. Indigestion: Stomach acupoint (FA-P 8) and Spleen acupoint (FA-P 10).

25. Diarrhea: Colon acupoint (FA-P 13) and Spleen acupoint (FA-P 10).

26. Pain in flank: Liver acupoint (FA-P 9).

27. Intercostal neuralgia: Chest acupoint (FA-P 3) and Liver acupoint (FA-P 9).

28. Lumbago: Kidney acupoint (FA-P 14), Ischium 1 acupoint (FA-P 18), Ischium 2 acupoint (FA-D 5), Lumbago acupoint (FA-D 4) and Waist and leg acupoint (FA-D 9).

29. Acute waist sprain: Lumbago acupoint (FA-D 4) and Waist and leg acupoint (FA-D 9).

30. Neuralgia sciatica: Ischium 1 acupoint (FA-P 18), Ischium 2 acupoint (FA-D 5), Waist and leg acupoint (FA-D 9) and Buttocks acupoint (FA-L 1).

31. Heart Palpitations: Heart acupoint (FA-P 5), Heart pain acupoint (FA-D 8) and Kidney acupoint (FA-P 14).

32. Asthma: Lung acupoint (FA-P 6), Chest acupoint (FA-P 3) and Heart pain acupoint (FA-D 8).

33. Chest pain: Chest acupoint (FA-P 3) and Lung acupoint (FA-P 6).

34. Peripheral neuritis: Zhiduan acupoint (FA-P 22).

35. Tumor pain: Aigen 1 acupoint (FA-P 12) and Aigen 2 acupoint (FA-P 17).

Chapter 5

OTHER FOOT THERAPIES

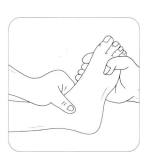

I. Foot Massage

An important branch of traditional Chinese medicine, traditional Chinese massage, also called Tuina (pushing and grasping) is an ancient therapy applied with physical stimulation.

The foot is a specific and compact structure of bones and thin muscles, rich in blood vessels and nerves. Therefore, the massage applied to the reflecting areas on the foot is quite different from that applied to other parts of the body.

1. Effects of massage:

(1) Balance of Yin and Yang and adjustment of internal organs: Massage at the reflecting areas can adjust the functions of their correspondent internal organs, promote the healing of injured organs, improve the body's resistance, and restore the normal functions of internal organs.

(2) Produce an effect from the body's surface to the internal organs, promote blood circulation and relieve blood stasis: Massage applied to the reflecting areas on the foot can cure diseases in their correspondent internal organs of the chest and abdominal cavities. It can also promote blood circulation, relieve blood stasis, and eliminate toxic pathogens.

(3) Relaxation of muscles and tranquilization of mind: Foot massage can relax the muscles originating from the toes.

(4) Treatment of diseases and preservation of health: Foot massage is a safe and effective treatment without harmful side effects.

2. Principles for selecting massage areas:

The reflecting areas on foot are selected for treatment according to the diseased organs and following the principles of holistics and differential diagnosis and treatment. They can be divided into basic, principal and supplemental areas.

(1) Basic areas: The basic areas can be used to enhance immunity

and improve the excretory function to discharge toxic and poisonous substance, including coeliac plexus, kidney, ureter and urinary
bladder areas. Massage on these areas should be repeated three
times before and after applying a whole massage set for either treatment of diseases or preservation of health.

(2) Principal areas: The reflecting areas of the diseased organs or
the injured parts of the body are the principal areas. Greater massage pressure, for a longer period of time, should be applied to
these areas. For example, the scapula, shoulder joint and trapezius
muscle areas are the principal areas for treating periarthritis of the
shoulder; and the uterus, ovary and vagina areas are the principal
areas where gynecological diseases occur.

(3) Supplemental areas: According to the nature of the disease and
the condition of the patient, supplemental areas are selected to
improve the therapeutic effect to the basic and principal areas. For
example, the spleen area may be used to treat hepatitis because
this liver disease may injure the spleen; the liver and kidney areas
may be selected to treat arthritis because the liver controls the tendons and the kidney controls the bones; and the lymph node areas
may be chosen to treat inflammatory diseases such as tossillitis and
bronchitis to enhance immunity.

3. Methods of massage:

The pad(s) of thumb and other fingers or the knuckles are used to
evenly and rhythmically apply pressure to the correspondent reflecting areas on the foot. The methods of massage include the following techniques:

(1) Pressing technique:

1) Pressing with tip of thumb: This is a common method, since the
thumb is soft, flexible, and has a wide range for massage. Pressure
is applied by repeatedly flexing and extending the joints of the
thumb. The other four fingers are put over the dorsum of foot while
the thumb is used to massage the sole; and they are placed over the

sole for application of nimble movement and firm pressure while the thumb massages the dorsum of the foot. The pressure is vertically applied with the tip of thumb 2-3 mm from the free edge of nail by flexing the interphalangeal joint of thumb to a rectangle and then extending it repeatedly. A series of continuous movements are gently and rhythmically applied to the reflecting areas (Fig. 25). This is a technique commonly used by beginners, but the long-lasting tension applied to the thumb during massage may cause tenosynovitis. Therefore, it may be used alternately with other techniques.

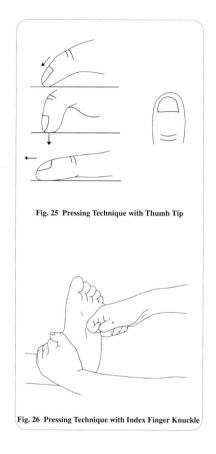

Fig. 25 Pressing Technique with Thumb Tip

Fig. 26 Pressing Technique with Index Finger Knuckle

2) Pressing with knuckle of index finger: The index finger is flexed and supported by the distal segment of thumb to apply a perpendicular pressure with the knuckle to the reflecting areas on foot with the hand, forearm, and upper arm arranged in a straight line. An even and penetrating force is applied and maintained for a while, and then released (Fig. 26). The pressing and releasing movement is then repeatedly performed for a period of time to produce a comfortable and tolerable sensation in the patient. This technique is

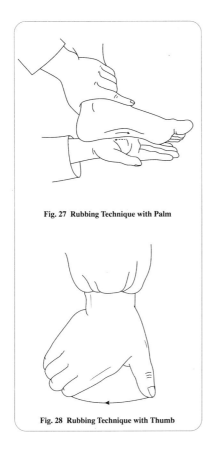

Fig. 27 Rubbing Technique with Palm

Fig. 28 Rubbing Technique with Thumb

usually applied to all reflecting areas on the sole and a few areas on other parts of the foot.

(2) Rubbing technique:

1) Rubbing with palm: This technique is usually applied at the beginning of foot massage treatment. The palm with all fingers extended and spread is used to press and rub the foot from heel to toes over all reflecting areas (Fig. 27) to relax the muscles, improve the functions of internal organs, and treat diseases.

2) Rubbing with thumb: The distal half of thumb pad is used to rub back and forth over a few nearby reflecting areas (Fig. 28). For example, from the kidney area to the ureter, urinary bladder, and colon areas.

(3) Kneading technique:

Only the distal half of thumb is used to do clockwise or counter-clockwise circular rotating movements over one reflecting area (Fig. 29), because it is comparatively small. The areas for applying the kneading technique such as the coeliac plexus and stomach areas, are larger than those where the pressing technique is applied.

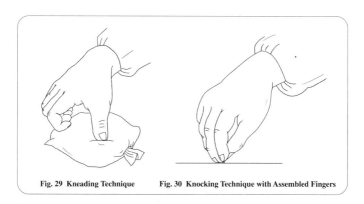

Fig. 29 Kneading Technique   Fig. 30 Knocking Technique with Assembled Fingers

(4) Knocking technique:

1) Knocking with index finger: The pads of thumb and index finger are placed together and the pad of middle finger is put on the nail of index finger. The protruding tip of index finger is then used to knock the reflecting areas on the sole or the dorsum of the foot while the hand moves up and down with the wrist joint as an axis.

2) Knocking with assembled fingers: The five fingers are slightly flexed with their distal segments assembled together in a plum-blossom shape and the fingers are then used to knock the reflecting areas with a spring force conducted from the wrist (Fig. 30). This technique is usually applied to the reflecting areas with thinner muscles, and is very useful in treating heel pain.

(5) Pinching technique:

The thumb and index finger are used to separately apply opposite pressing and kneading techniques to two reflecting areas (Fig. 31). Otherwise, the index is used as a fixed finger placed on a reflecting area, and then a pressing and kneading technique is applied to an opposite area by the thumb over the index finger. This technique is usually applied to two opposite reflecting areas, such as those of the lower lymph nodes.

60

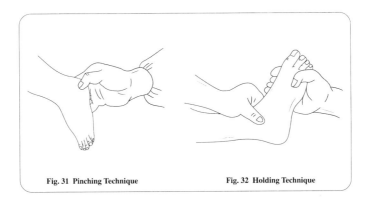

Fig. 31 Pinching Technique   Fig. 32 Holding Technique

(6) Holding technique:

Opposite the thumb, the four other fingers are put on several corre-lated reflecting areas to hold the foot and simultaneously apply pres-sure to those areas, such as the thoracic and lumbar spine and sacrum areas, or eye, ear, and nose areas (Fig. 32) for treatment of disease or health maintenance.

Remarks:

1. Rhythm of massage: Massage rhythm when applying pressure may vary according to the nature of the disease and condition of the patient. For example, frequency should be longer for weak pa-tient and shorter for stronger patients.

2. Pressure of massage: Pressure should be lower for weak patients and may be higher for stronger patients. A pressing force producing a moderate local pain is a proper pressure. Severe pain should al-ways be avoided.

3. Amount of stimulation: The amount of stimulation can be di-vided into light and heavy. At the start of the massage, stimulation should be applied gently. Intensity may be gradually increased, and then reduced to its initial gentleness before finishing the massage. After an increase of the patient's tolerance, more intensive stimula-tion may be applied.

4. Time of massage: The duration of the massage to a particular area may vary from 20 to 50 seconds depending on the nature of the reflecting areas and the condition of the patient. The duration of a massage applied to principal areas should be longer, and the total time for a massage of both feet is about 30-40 minutes, once a day or every other day. A therapeutic course consists of ten treatments, and a rest of one to two days is recommended between courses of treatment.

II. Foot Acupuncture

1. Effects of foot acupuncture:

(1) Adjustment of Yin and Yang: Diseases may be cured by foot acupuncture through the adjustment of Yin and Yang deficiency to restore the normal physiological functions of the body.
(2) Improvement of body resistance and the discharge of pathogens.
(3) Release of stasis of meridians.
According to the mechanism of exchange between physiological and pathological processes in the meridians and internal organs, the acupuncture and moxibustion applied at acupoints may eliminate the pathogenic factors and cure the diseases.

2. Principles for selecting acupoints:

(1) Selection of nearby acupoints: The local or nearby acupoints are usually selected to treat localized lesions with symptoms such as redness, swelling, pain and numbness from either acute or chronic diseases. For example, Shangqiu (SP 5), Qiuxu (GB 40) and Jiexi (ST 41) can be used to treat ankle joint pain.
(2) Selection of remote acupoints: The remote acupoints may be selected according to the theory of meridians and internal organs. For example, Gongsun (SP 4) can be used to treat stomachache, and Zhiyin (BL 67) can be selected to treat diseases of the head and

face.

(3) Selection of acupoints according to the nature of the diseases and the specific function of the acupoints: Taichong (LR 3) can be used to treat stagnation of liver qi, and Jiexi (ST 41) can be used to relieve stomachache.

3. Foot acupuncture methods:

(1) Preparation before acupuncture: The quality of the needles should be checked before application of acupuncture. The handle of the needles should be firmly welded to the trunk, and the trunk should be straight, smooth, firm and elastic. The tip of the needle should be as sharp as a pine needle. Needles with defects should be discarded. Needles of different lengths and thicknesses are used according to the location of acupoints as well as the physique and physical condition of the patient.

(2) Posture selection: The patient's posture when receiving foot acupuncture is very important for the correct localization of the acupoints, the proper insertion and manipulation of the needles, and the prevention of fainting and needle mishaps. In the proper posture, the patient may comfortably keep his body still for a long time and the practitioner can correctly locate the acupoints and conveniently apply acupuncture. The common postures for foot acupuncture are the following:

Supine lying posture: Convenient for application of acupuncture to the dorsal side of foot.

Lying on side posture: Convenient for application of acupuncture to lateral side of foot.

Prone lying posture: Convenient for application of acupuncture to plantar side of foot.

(3) Sterilization: The acupuncture instruments are sterilized in an autoclave or by boiling or soaking in alcohol. The needles used for patients with infectious diseases should be strictly sterilized and stored separately. The skin and hands of the practitioner may be

sterilized with alcohol cotton balls.

(4) Insertion of needle: To insert the needle, the left thumb placed near the acupoint to press the skin, and the needle is held by the right hand and inserted into the acupoint along the nail of the left thumb. Strong stimulation may be applied to patients with excessive syndrome, and weak stimulation may be applied to patients with deficient syndrome. The needle may be retained in place for 10 to 20 minutes and then removed, and a sterilized cotton ball is then placed over the puncture hole.

(5) Application of moxibustion: The burned end of a moxa roll is put 2 cm above the acupoint for 3 to 5 minutes until the local skin is flushed. Burn injuries to the skin must be carefully avoided.

III. Application of Drugs on Foot

Different combinations of drugs made of Chinese herbs are applied over the reflecting areas and acupoints of foot to treat diseases.

1. Effects of this Treatment:
The local application of drugs may produce a direct stimulation to the reflecting areas and acupoints or have an indirect therapeutic effect on the body after they are absorbed through the skin to resolve inflammation and swelling, expel cold and damp pathogens, and relieve pain and fatigue.

2. Principles for selecting acupoints:
(1) According to location of lesion: The lesion's reflecting areas on the foot may be selected for treatment. For example, the eye (8) area is used to treat eye diseases; and the lung and bronchus (14) area is used to treat coughs and asthma.

(2) According to traditional Chinese medical theory: The theories of meridians and internal organs and the change of physiological

and pathological functions are also bases for selecting acupoints. For example, the acupoints of the gallbladder meridian are used to treat migraine because it passes through the lateral side of the head, and the acupoints of the liver meridian are used to treat redness, swelling and pain of eyes because the eye is the external orifice of the liver.

(3) According to the precepts of modern medicine: The pituitary gland (4) area is used to treat irregular menstruation; and the adrenal gland (21) area is used to treat reactions to fluid infusion.

3. Treatment methods:

Because fresh plant herbs contain juice, after pounding an herbal paste may be directly applied over the reflecting areas and acupoints. Dry herbs must be ground to prepare powder first and then mixed with excipients (alcohol, vinegar, water, ginger juice, egg white or bee honey) to produce a paste for application. The methods of preparing external drugs are very simple, and patients often can prepare the drugs for themselves.

(1) Herbal powder: Prescription herbs are mixed up and ground to prepare a powder, which is then stored in a container and put in a cool, dark place.

Before application, the powder is mixed with water or other excipients to prepare small cakes or pills which are applied and fixed with adhesive plaster on the reflecting areas or acupoints of the foot.

(2) Herbal pills: Prescription herbal powder is mixed with alcohol, vinegar, egg white, or honey to prepare pills of different sizes according to the size of the reflecting areas and acupoints. These pills are usually applied and fixed with adhesive plaster on small reflecting areas and acupoints.

(3) Herbal paste: Prescription fresh plant herbs may be pounded to directly prepare a paste. Dry herbal powder may be mixed with alcohol, vinegar, egg white or honey to prepare a paste for applica-

tion over the reflecting areas or acupoints in an even thickness and shapes the same as the reflecting areas to produce a long-lasting therapeutic effect by the slow absorption of the herbs.

(4) Herbal ointment: Prescription herbal powder is evenly mixed with an excipient and fried in a pot to prepare an ointment for application over the reflecting areas or acupoints of the foot.

Herbal ointment is easily spread and affixed to the skin, and the herbal ingredients in the ointment are easily absorbed through the skin.

(5) Herbal cakes: Prescription herbal powder and wheat flour are mixed with water to prepare small cakes. After steaming, the hot cakes are applied over the reflecting areas or acupoints. The penetration of the herbal ingredients from the hot cakes is very effective in producing good therapeutic results.

(6) Herbal decoction: Prescription herbs are soaked in warm water for half an hour, then boiled over a strong fire until the volume of water is reduced to one half the original amount, and then boiled again on a low flame. A wet compress of the hot herbal decoction soaked in soft cloth or gauze is applied over the reflecting areas or acupoints to promote blood circulation, relax muscles, and moisten the skin. The skin always should be carefully protected from burn injuries.

Cautions:

1. The above methods are contraindicated for patients who are allergic to herbs.

2. They are also contraindicated for patients with severe ulceration, erosion, and trauma of the foot skin.

3. Patients with acute abdominal conditions that may require surgery should not be treated with the above methods.

IV. Foot Bath

An external traditional Chinese therapy, the foot bath includes both steaming and washing methods.

In the steaming method, the feet are placed in steam evaporated from a boiled herbal decoction for the treatment of disease, and in the washing method, the feet are soaked in a warm herbal decoction for treatment. Both methods are mentioned in many ancient medical books.

1. Effects of foot bath:

A long foot bath can produce both a local therapeutic and thermal effect and a remote therapeutic effect through qi, blood and the meridians from the body surface to the internal organs, and from the lower to upper part of the body for adjustment of qi, blood, Yin and Yang, the reinforcement of body resistance, and the removal of pathogens.

2. Foot bath methods:

The steaming and washing methods may be flexibly applied independently, jointly, or alternately.

Steaming method: A boiled herbal decoction is poured into a container to one-half or two-thirds full and the patient's feet are put over the hot fluid and covered with a towel to preserve the warmth.

Washing method: A warm herbal decoction with the herb residue discarded is used to soak and wash both feet. This method can be used alone or after the steaming method.

The foot bath may be applied for 30 minutes, one or twice a day.

The foot bath can be used to treat tinea, swelling of limbs caused by trauma, pain, common cold without sweating, beriberi affecting the heart, difficult urination, prolapse of rectum or uterus, rheumatism, disturbance of periperal blood vessels, diseases of locomotive system, obesity, cutaneous pruritus, and Guillain-Barre syndrome.

3. Precautions:

(1) For steaming therapy, the distance of feet above the hot liquid may be adjusted according to the temperature of the decoction to obtain a comfortable sensation, not burning the feet.

(2) An adequate temperature for the warm herbal decoction in washing therapy is about 40 degrees centigrade.

(3) After foot bath, the feet should be wiped dry and the warmth of feet preserved to avoid an attack of wind and cold.

(4) The foot bath must not be used to treat patients with malignant tumors, epilepsy, acute inflammation, heart failure, and chronic pulmonary heart disease.

Chapter 6

TREATMENT OF COMMON DISEASES

I. Medical Diseases

1. Common cold (influenza):

This is a common infectious disease caused by an attack of external wind pathogens.

Differential diagnosis: Patients with common cold due to wind and cold pathogens may suffer from nasal obstruction, dull voice, sneezing, running nose with clear discharge, itching in throat, cough with profuse thin sputum, severe chills, low fever, headache, pain in body, no sweating, thin and white tongue coating, and slow pulse. Patients with colds due to wind and heat pathogens may suffer from high fever, mild chills, sweating, headache or dizziness, nasal obstruction, running nose, flushed face, red eyes, thirst and dryness in mouth, sore throat, cough with yellow sticky sputum difficult to spit out, chest distress, thin and yellow tongue coating, and rapid pulse. Patients with colds due to dampness may suffer from chills, fever, body heat not relievable by sweating, heaviness and body fatigue, dizziness, cough with white sticky sputum, distension of chest and abdomen, loose stool, scanty and yellow urine, white and greasy or yellow and greasy tongue coating, and soft and rapid pulse.

Treatment:

(1) Foot massage:

Foot massage is applied on head 1, cerebellum 3, throat 48, tonsil 45 and nose 6 reflecting areas (Fig. 33).

(2) Foot acupuncture:

1) Meridianal acupoints: At Kunlun (BL 60), Jiexi (ST 41), Zutonggu (BL 66), Zhaohai (KI 6) and Rangu (KI 2), the reducing technique is applied and the needles are retained for 20 minutes; moxibustion is applied after acupuncture in patients with cold or damp pathogens.

2) Extra acupoints: At Dazhi Jumao (EX-F 14), Zuxin (EX-F 18) and Bafeng (EX-F 22), the reducing technique is applied and the needles are retained for 20 minutes; moxibustion is applied after acupunc-

70

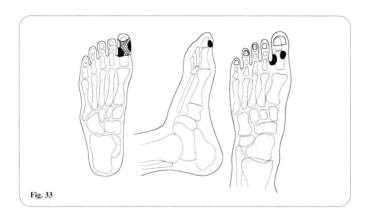

Fig. 33

ture in patients with cold or damp pathogens.

3) Foot acupoints: At Head and face (FA-P 1), Kidney (FA-P 14) and Heart pain (FA-D 8) acupoints, a moderate twisting stimulation is applied and the needles are retained for 20 minutes.

(3) External application of drugs:

1) The powder of Baijiezi (white mustard seed) 9 gm is mixed with the whites of two eggs to prepare a paste for application over the sole.

2) The powder of Tiannanxing (raw Jack-in-the-pulpit tuber) 31 gm is mixed with vinegar to prepare a paste for application over the central area of both soles.

3) An adequate amount of Baifan (alum) and wheat flour is mixed with vinegar or boiled water to prepare a paste for application over Yongquan (KI 1) acupoint.

2. Cough:

The cough is a common symptom of respiratory diseases.

Differential diagnosis: Patients with cough due to cold pathogens may suffer from cough with white and thin sputum, fever, chills, pale tongue with thin and white coating, or slow pulse. Patients with colds due to heat pathogens may suffer from cough with yellow and sticky sputum difficult to spit out, sore throat, pale tongue with thin and yellow coating, and rapid pulse. Patients with colds due to damp pathogens may suffer from severe cough in the morning, sticky sputum or thin and white or dark and grey sputum difficult to spit out at the early stage of cough, but easy to spit out after relief of cough, pale and puffy tongue with white and greasy coating, and soft or rolling pulse. And patients with liver fire may suffer from paroxymal cough with scanty and sticky sputum and stretching pain in chest and flank exacerbated by emotional disturbance and anger, slightly flushed face, dryness in throat and bitter taste in mouth, red tip of tongue, thin and yellow coating, or wiry and rapid pulse. Cough in patients with tracheitis, bronchitis or pneumonia may be treated by the following methods.

Treatment:

(1) Foot massage:

The foot massage is applied on larynx, trachea, vocal cord 48, lung and bronchus 14, lymph nodes (chest, 41), kidney 22 and spleen

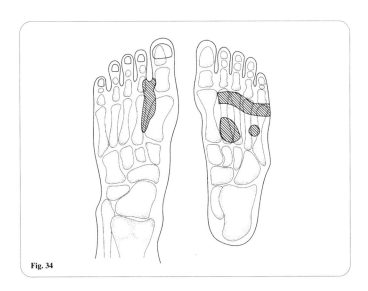

Fig. 34

72

34 reflecting areas (Fig. 34).

(2) Foot acupuncture:

1) Meridianal acupoints: At Zuqiaoyin (GB 44), Zutonggu (BL 66), Yongquan (KI 1), Taixi (KI 3) and Dazhong (KI 4) and at Lidui (ST 45), Neiting (ST 44), Chongyang (ST 42) and Xian'gu (ST 43) for patients with fever, the reducing technique is applied; and acupuncture plus moxibustion is applied for patients with severe cold or dampness.

2) Foot acupoints: At Lung acupoint (FA-P 6), a moderate twisting stimulation is applied and the needle is retained for 20 minutes; Spleen (FA-P 10) and Stomach (FA-P 8) acupoints may be added for patients with damp pathogens; Liver acupoint (FA-P 9) may be added for patients with liver fire, and the moxibustion after acupuncture may be applied for patients with severe damp pathogens.

(3) External application of drugs:

The powder of Baihujiao (white pepper) 7 grains, Zhizi (cape-jasmine fruit) 6 gm, Taoren (peach pit) 7 pieces, Xinren (almond) 7 pieces, and sticky rice 7 grains is mixed with egg white to prepare a paste for application over the sole at night and removal the next morning.

3. Pulmonary Tuberculosis:

This is a chronic infectious disease caused by tuberculous bacilli with cough, hemoptysis, tidal fever, night sweating, and pathological leanness.

Differential diagnosis: Patients with lung deficiency may suffer from dry cough with scanty sticky sputum, blood in sputum, chest distress and dull pain, dryness of mouth and throat, hot palms and soles, fatigue, red tongue with thin and white coating, and thready and rapid pulse. Patients with spleen deficiency may suffer from cough with profuse sputum, blood streaks in thin sputum, spontaneous sweating during the day, loss of appetite, diarrhea, pale complexion, pale tongue with scanty coating, and thready and weak pulse. Patients with kidney deficiency may suffer from severe cough with scanty sticky sputum, hemoptysis of blood, pain in sternum while coughing, flushed cheeks, annoyance, thirst, insomnia, emission of semen, amenorrhea, red and bared tongue without coating or with thin and yellow coating, and thready and rapid pulse.

Treatment:

(1) Foot massage:

Foot massage is applied to lung and bronchus 14, larynx, trachea, vocal cord 48, lymph nodes (chest, 41), spleen 34, kidney 22, lymph nodes (upper body, 39) and lymph nodes (abdomen, 40) reflecting areas (Fig. 35).

(2) Foot acupuncture:

1) Meridianal acupoints: At Zuqiaoyin (GB 44), Zutonggu (BL 66), Neiting (ST 44), Taixi (KI 3) and Rangu (KI 2), the reinforcing technique is applied and the needles are retained for 20 minutes; Dazhong (KI 4) is added for patients with hemoptysis; and moxibustion is applied after acupuncture for patients with spleen deficiency.

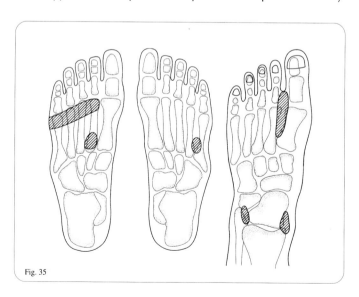

Fig. 35

2) Foot acupoints: At Chest (FA-P 3) and Lung (FA-P 6) acupoints, a moderate twisting stimulation is applied and the needles are retained for 20 minutes. Spleen (FA-P 10) and Stomach and intestine (FA-D 7) acupoints are added for patients with spleen deficiency; and Kidney (FA-P 14) and Anmian (FA-P 2) acupoints are added for patients with kidney deficiency.

(3) External application of drugs:

The Dahuang (rhubarb) 10 gm, Liuhuang (sulfur powder) 6 gm, Rougui (cinnamon bark powder) 3 gm and Bingpian (borneol) 3 gm are pounded with fresh garlic to prepare a paste for application over bilateral Yongquan (KI 1) acupoints after spreading on a piece of gauze that should be changed every other day.

4. Asthma:

Asthma is an allergic condition with paroxysmal attacks of chest distress and shortness of breath including wheezing and orthopnea. Before the attack, the patient may have some prodromal symptoms such as itching in throat, sneezing, coughing and chest distress.

Differential diagnosis: Patients with asthma caused by wind and cold pathogens may suffer from shortness of breath and chest distress exacerbated by attack of cold, chills, fever, running nose, pink tongue with white and slippery coating, and floating and slow pulse. Patients with asthma caused by wind and heat pathogens may suffer from chest distress, yellow and sticky sputum difficult to spit out, thirst, red tongue with yellow and greasy coating, and rolling and rapid pulse. Patients with excessive phlegm may suffer from profuse and sticky sputum difficult to spit out, chest distress, poor appetite, white and greasy tongue coating, and rolling pulse. Patients with lung deficiency may suffer from shortness of breath, low and weak coughing, dry mouth, red tongue, and thready and weak pulse; and patients with kidney deficiency may suffer from chronic asthma with short inspiration and long expiration, leanness of body, cold limbs, edema of limbs, difficult urination, heart palpitations, pale tongue, and deep and thready pulse. Asthma and shortness of breath in patients with bronchial asthma, asthmatic bronchitis, pneumonia, cardiac asthma, obstructive emphysema and hysteria in modern medicine may be treated by the following methods.

Treatment:

(1) Foot massage:

Foot massage is applied to larynx, trachea, vocal cord 48, lung and bronchus 14, lymph nodes (chest, 41), parathyroid gland 13, kidney 22, spleen 34 and adrenal gland 21 reflecting areas (Fig. 36).

(2) Foot acupuncture:

1) Meridianal acupoints: At Zulinqi (GB 41), Kunlun (BL 60), Zutonggu (BL 66), Yinbai (SP 1), Yongquan (KI 1) and Rangu (KI 2), the reducing technique is applied and the needles are retained for 20 minutes. Warm acupuncture may be applied for patients with wind and cold pathogens, damp pathogens or kidney deficiency.

2) Foot acupoints: At Chest (FA-P 3), Aigen 3 (FA-P 7) and Heart pain (FA-D 8) acupoints, a moderate twisting stimulation is applied and the needles are retained for 20 minutes. Kidney (FA-P 14) acupoint may be added for patients with kidney deficiency, and

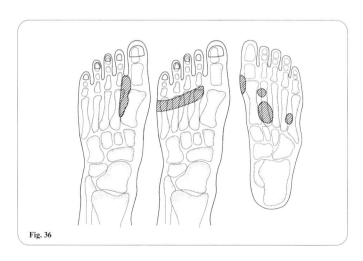

Fig. 36

76

moxibustion after acupuncture is applied to patients with cold pathogens, turbid phlegm or kidney deficiency.

(3) External application of drugs:

1) Baifan (alum) 30 gm and an adequate amount of wheat flour and vinegar are mixed to prepare small cakes for overnight application on the central area of both soles.

2) Baifan (alum) 30 gm is mixed with vinegar to prepare a paste for application once a day over the central area of both soles.

(4) Foot bath:

Two eggs are boiled in a decoction of the following herbs: Yuxingcao (houttuynia) 60 gm, Zisuzi (perilla fruit) 30 gm, Wuweizi (magnoliavine fruit) 20 gm, Dilong (dry earthworm) 30 gm and Chenxiang (eagle wood) 10 gm for 30 minutes. The eggs are then eaten and the decoction is used to soak and wash both feet once a night.

5. Heat stroke:

Heat stroke is an acute condition occurring in very hot weather. Its symptoms include high fever with little or no sweating, pale complexion, hot or wet and cold skin, restlessness, apathy, nausea, vomiting, hypotension, thready and weak and rapid pulse, mental confusion, and muscle spasm. Heat cramps, heat exhaustion, heat stroke, and sun stroke in modern medicine can be treated by the following methods.

Treatment:

(1) Foot massage:

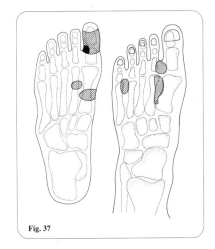

Fig. 37

Foot massage can be applied to the head 1, brain stem and cerebellum 3, lymph nodes (chest, 41), stomach 15, adrenal gland 21 and balance organ (labyrinth, 42) reflecting areas (Fig. 37).

(2) Foot acupuncture:

1) Meridianal acupoints: At Jiexi (ST 41), Neiting (ST 44), Yongquan (KI 1) and Zutonggu (BL 66), strong stimulation with reducing and twisting technique is applied for 5 minutes and repeated after an interval of 3-5 minutes through the needle-retention period of 30 minutes. Moxibustion is applied to Yongquan (KI 1) for patients with hypotension.

2) Extra acupoints: At Zuxin (EX-F 18), Dazhi Jumao (EX-F 14), Xiaozhijian (tip of little toe) and Qiduan (EX-F 23), a strong reducing technique is applied and the needles are retained for 20 minutes.

6. Hypertension:

The critical clinical manifestation of hypertensive disease is the elevation of arterial blood pressure above 21.3/12.7 kPa.

Differential diagnosis: Patients with excessive liver fire may suffer from headache, vertigo, flushed face, red eyes, bitter taste in mouth, dry throat, impatience, anger, constipation, short stream of dark urine, red tongue with yellow coating, and thready and rapid pulse. Patients with turbid phlegm may suffer from vertigo, fullness and distension of upper abdomen, vomiting of sputum and saliva, poor appetite, heaviness and fatigue of limbs, white and greasy tongue coating, and wiry and rolling pulse. Patients with Yin deficiency and excessive Yang may suffer from tinnitus, vertigo, head heaviness and weakness of legs, impatience, anger, annoyance, insomnia, soreness of waist and weakness of legs, numbness of limbs, hand and foot tremor, red tongue with scanty coating and wiry and thready pulse. Patients with Yin deficiency may suffer from heat in palms and soles, dry mouth and throat, red and dry tongue with scanty coating, and wiry, thready and rapid pulse. And patients with Yang deficiency may suffer from aversion to cold, cold limbs, long streams of clear urine, diarrhea, edema of lower limbs, pale tongue, and deep and thready pulse.

Treatment:

(1) Foot massage:

Massage is applied to head 1, brain stem and cerebellum 3, kidney 22, liver 18, gallbladder 19, heart 33, urinary bladder 24 and balance organ (labyrinth, 42) reflecting areas (Fig. 38).

(2) Foot acupuncture:

1) Meridianal acupoints: At Jiexi (ST 41), Taichong (LR 3), Xingjian (LR 2), Kunlun (BL 60), Shenmai (BL 62) and Xiaxi (GB 43) acupoints, the balanced reinforce-reducing technique is applied and the needles are retained for 20 minutes. Zhaohai (KI 6) is added for thirst and dry throat; Zuqiaoyin (GB 44) is added for tinnitus and deafness; and Jiexi (ST 41) and Dazhong (KI 4) are added for constipation.

2) Extra acupoints: At Dazhi Jumao (EX-F 14), Xiaozhijian (tip of little toe) and Zuxin (EX-F 18), the balanced reinforce-reducing technique is applied and the needles are retained for 20 minutes, and

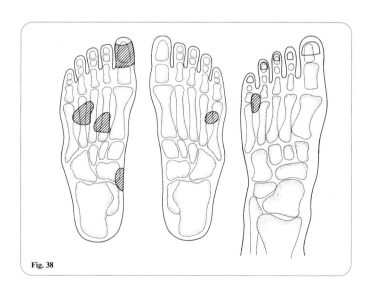

Fig. 38

moxibustion after acupuncture is applied for patients with turbid phlegm and Yang deficiency.

3) Foot acupoints: At Heart (FA-P 5), Kidney (FA-P 14) and Vertigo (FA-M 1) acupoints, a moderate twisting stimulation is applied and the needles are retained for 20 minutes.

(3) External application of drugs:

1) Wuzhuyu pounder (evodia fruit) 5 gm and Chuanxiong 5 gm is mixed with egg white to prepare a paste for application to Head 1 and Yongquan (KI 1) reflecting areas after it is spread on sulfuric acid paper, which is affixed with adhesive plaster.

2) The Kuguateng (bitter gourd vine) 10 gm and a handful of Denglongpao (Gooseberry) are pounded to prepare a paste for application to Head 1 and Brain stem and cerebellum 3 reflecting areas.

(4) Foot bath:

A warm decoction of 1500 ml of Chongweizi (Chinese mother-wort) 10-15 gm, Sangshupi (mulberry bark) 10-15 gm and Sangye (mulberry leaf) 10-15 gm in a basin is used to soak the feet for 30 minutes. A hypotensive effect may appear after soaking the feet for 30 minutes. This effect may reach a peak one hour later and last for 4 to 6 hours. Blood pressure may be reduced to normal after one or two foot bath treatments.

7. Hemiplegia:

Hemiplegia is a condition which includes impairment of movement or paralysis of the limbs on one side, most commonly found in aged people with a history of hypertension and arteriosclerosis. Differential diagnosis: Patients with a depletion of collaterals and blood vessels may suffer from weakness of the limbs, numbness of skin, muscles, hands and feet, sudden onset of deviation of mouth and eyes, slurred speech, drooling, edema of hands and feet, poor appetite, incontinence of urine and stool, sallow or dull complexion, thin and white tongue coating, and floating and rapid pulse. Patients afflicted with upward disturbance of wind and Yang may suffer from stiff limbs, muscle contractions, tinnitus, vertigo, insomnia, dreaminess, bitter taste in mouth, dry throat, flushed face, short streams of dark urine, constipation, dark red tongue with thin and yellow coating, and hard and strong pulse. Patients with cerebral hemorrhage, cerebral thrombosis, cerebral embolism, spasm of cerebral artery, subarachnoid hemorrhage, and other cerebrovascular diseases recognized by modern medicine as hemiplegia can be treated by the following methods.

Treatment:

(1) Foot massage:

The massage is applied to head 1, frontal sinus 2, brain stem and cerebellum 3, shoulder 10, hip joint 38, pituitary gland 4, adrenal gland 21, kidney 22, heart 33, spleen 34, knee 35 and elbow joint 60 reflecting areas (Fig. 39).

(2) Foot acupuncture:

1) Meridianal acupoints: At Jiexi (ST 41), Lidui (ST 45), Qiuxu (GB 40), Kunlun (BL 60), Pucan (BL 61), Shenmai (BL 62) and Yongquan

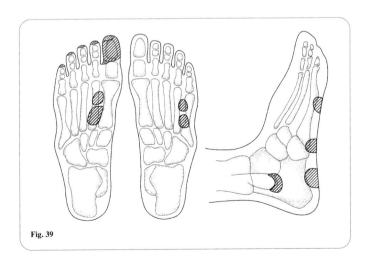

Fig. 39

(KI 1) acupoints the balanced reinforce-reducing technique is applied and the needles are retained for 20 minutes; moxibustion after acupuncture is applied for patients with a depletion of collaterals and blood vessels.

2) Extra acupoints: At Xiakunlun (EX-F 3) and Dazhi Jumao (EX-F 14) acupoints, the balanced reinforce-reducing technique is applied and the needles are retained for 20 minutes; moxibustion after acupuncture is applied to patients with a depletion of collaterals and blood vessels.

(3) External application of drugs:

1) The powder of Quanxie (whole scorpion) 1 piece, Danshen (red sageroot) 5 gm, Yanhusuo (corydalis tuber) 5 gm and Danpi (peony bark) 5 gm is mixed with liquor and spread on sulfuric acid paper for application on the central area of both soles and affixed with adhesive plaster.

2) The powder of Taoren (peach kernel) 5 pieces, Zhizi (cape-jasmine fruit) 5 pieces and Shexiang (musk) 0.2 gm is mixed and applied over the left sole for men and right sole for women and affixed with adhesive plaster and changed once every three days. Spicy food is prohibited for these patients.

(4) Foot bath:

For patients with apoplexy including muscle contractions of hands and feet, Shenjincao (club-moss) 3 gm, Tougucao (spermakia) 3 gm and Honghua (safflower) 3 gm are boiled in a basin with 2 kg of water for 10 minutes and the warm decoction of 50-60 degrees centigrade is used to soak and wash the hands first and then the feet for 15 to 20 minutes 3 times a day. The decoction may be reheated if it becomes cool and the fingers and toes may move freely in the decoction.

8. Facial palsy:

This is a condition caused by the inflammation of facial nerves producing deviation of mouth and eye and drooling. Facial paralysis

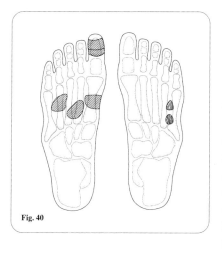

Fig. 40

caused by cerebral hemorrhage, cerebral thrombosis, other cerebrovascular accidents, profuse hemorrhage, otitis media, parotitis, rheumatic neuritis of facial nerve, periostitis of stylomastoid foramen, and herpes zoster recognized by modern medicine may be treated by the following methods.

Treatment:

(1) Foot massage:

The massage may be applied to trigeminal nerve 5, head 1, ear 9, frontal sinus 2, liver 18, spleen 34, kidney 22 and eye 8 reflecting areas (Fig. 40).

(2) Foot acupuncture:

1) Meridianal acupoints: At Lidui (ST 45), Chongyang (ST 42), Xingjian (LR 2) and Taichong (LR 3) acupoints, the reducing technique is applied and the needles are retained for 20 minutes.

2) Foot acupoints: At Head and face (FA-P 1) and Face (FA-P 4) acupoints, a moderate twisting stimulation is applied and the needles are retained for 20 minutes.

9. Facial spasm:

This is a condition of the facial muscles including automatic, irregular and paroxysmal spasms or twitching, often induced by nervousness and emotional distress.

Differential diagnosis: Patients suffering from an attack of liver wind to the face may suffer from high irritability, anger, distension and pain in both costal regions, belching, sighing, exacerbation of facial spasms during emotional turmoil, pale tongue with white coating, and wiry pulse. Patients with an upward flaming of heart fire may suffer from mental depression, anxiety, reduction of appetite, insomnia, dreaminess, red tip of tongue with yellow coating, and thready and rapid pulse. And patients with qi and blood deficiency may suffer from weakness of the entire body, reduction of appetite, weight loss, exacerbation of facial spasms or twitching after heavy mental activity, pale tongue with thin and white coating, and thready and weak pulse. Facial spasms caused by mental disturbance or secondary to facial palsy, trigeminal neuralgia, encephalitis-B, epidemic meningitis, and cerebrovascular diseases recognized by modern medicine may be treated by the following methods.

Treatment:

(1) Foot massage:

The massage can be applied to trigeminal nerve 5, head 1, liver 18, heart 33, spleen 34, kidney 22 and stomach 15 reflecting areas (Fig. 41).

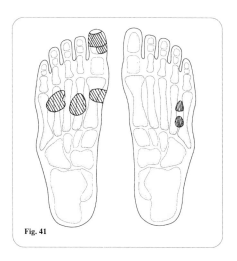

Fig. 41

(2) Foot acupuncture:

1) Meridianal acupoints: At Zhiyin (BL 67), Lidui (ST 45), Xiaxi (GB 43) and Zuqiaoyin (GB 44) acupoints the reducing technique is applied to patients of the first two types, and the reinforcing technique is applied to patients of the last type with moxibustion after acupuncture.

2) Foot acupoints: At Face (FA-P 4) and Head and face (FA-P 1)

acupoints, moderate twisting stimulation is applied. The Heart (FA-P 5) may be added to treat upward flaming of heart fire; and the Liver (FA-P 9) acupoint may be added to treat attack of liver wind to the face.

10. Insomnia:

Insomnia is the condition of sleeplessness caused by spiritual irritation, mental fatigue, general weakness after chronic disease or improper diet. In mild insomnia, the patient may have difficulty falling asleep, is easily awakened and has difficulty falling asleep again, or is awakened repeatedly; in severe insomnia, the patient cannot fall asleep at all.

Differential diagnosis: Patients with heart and spleen deficiency may suffer from dreaminess, uneasy sleep, heat palpitations, poor memory, mental fatigue, weakness, poor appetite, sallow complexion, pale tongue with thin coating, and thready and weak pulse. Patients with Yin deficiency and excessive fire may suffer from ann-oyance, insomnia, dizziness, tinnitus, dryness in mouth with scanty saliva, hotness in heart, palms, and soles, emission of semen with sexual dreams, poor memory, heart palpitations, lumbago, red tongue, and thready and rapid pulse. Patients afflicted by internal disturbance of heat and phlegm may suffer from insomnia, vertigo, chest distress, heaviness of head, annoyance, bitter taste in mouth, sallow complexion, greasy tongue coating, and rolling and rapid pulse. Neurasthenia and menopausal syndrome with severe insomnia recognized by modern medicine can be treated by the following methods.

Treatment:

(1) Foot massage:

The massage can be applied to frontal sinus 2, parathyroid gland 13, head 1, brain stem and cerebellum 3, thyroid gland 12, spleen 34 and kidney 22 reflecting areas (Fig. 42).

(2) Foot acupunture:

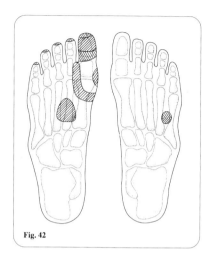

Fig. 42

1) Meridianal acupoints: At Shenmai (BL 62), Zhaohai (KI 6), Xingjian (LR 2) and Taichong (LR 3) acupoints, the reinforcing technique may be applied to patients of the first two types, and the reducing technique may be applied to patients of last type, and the needles may be retained for 40 minutes. Moxibustion after acupuncture may be applied to patients with heart and spleen deficiency.

2) Extra acupoints: At Insomnia (EX-F 8), Zuxin (EX-F 18) and Xiaozhijian (tip of little toe) acupoints, moderate lifting, thrusting and twisting stimulation may be applied with the needles retained for 40 minutes, and moxibustion after acupuncture may be applied to patients with heart and spleen deficiency.

3) Foot acupoints: At Anmian (FA-P 2), Heart (FA-P 5), Stomach (FA-P 8) and Spleen (FA-P 10) acupoints a strong twisting stimulation may be applied and the needles retained for 30 minutes.

(3) External application of drug:

The Wuzhuyu (evodia fruit) 9 gm is pounded with an adequate amount of vinegar to prepare a paste for application over bilateral Yongquan (KI 1) for 24 hours.

(4) Foot bath:

Patients are asked to take a foot bath with warm water for 10 minutes before going to bed each night.

11. Heart palpitations:

Patients may have unrelieved heart palpitations due to uncontrollable fear.

Differential diagnosis: Patients with heart qi deficiency may suffer from fear, insomnia, dreaminess, pale tongue with thin and white coating, and feeble pulse. Patients with deficiency of heart blood may suffer from dizziness, sallow complexion, fatigue, pale tongue with thin and white coating, and weak pulse. Patients with heart Yin deficiency may suffer from annoyance, insomnia, dizziness, hotness in palms and soles, tinnitus, red tongue with thin and white or thin and yellow coating, and thready and rapid pulse. Patients with heart Yang deficiency may suffer from chest distress, shortness of breath, pale complexion, cold body and limbs, pale tongue with thin, white and slippery coating, and feeble and weak pulse. Patients with stasis of heart blood may suffer from chest distress, occasional precordinal pain, cyanosis of lips and nails, and dark purple tongue. Patients with deficiency of spleen and kidney Yang may suffer from distension of upper abdomen, reduced amount of urine, edema of lower limbs, thirst without desire to drink water, white and slippery tongue coating, and wiry and rolling pulse. Arrhythmia of different heart diseases and heart palpitations in iron deficiency anemia, aplastic anemia, hypothyroidism and neurasthenia recognized by modern medicine can be treated by the following methods.

Treatment:

(1) Foot massage:

The massage may be applied to the heart 33, kidney 22, spleen 34, head 1, thyroid gland 12 and adrenal gland 21 reflecting areas (Fig. 43).

(2) Foot acupuncture:

1) Meridianal acupoints: Zulinqi (GB 41), Shenmai (BL 62), Jinggu (BL 64), Taibai (SP 3) and Rangu (KI 2) are used; Xiangu (ST 43) and Neiting (ST 44) are added for patients with edema of lower limbs;

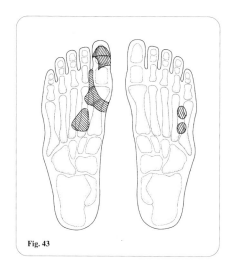

Fig. 43

the reinforcing technique of acupuncture is applied with moxibustion for patients with deficiency of heart qi, unsteady heart blood and heart Yang; the balanced reinforce-reducing technique is applied to patients with heart Yin deficiency; and the reducing technique is applied to patients with heart blood stasis. The needles are retained for 20 minutes.

2) Foot acupoints: At Heart (FA-P 5), Heart pain (FA-D 8) and Neizhiyin (EX-F 20) acupoint, a moderate twisting stimulation is applied and the needles are retained for 20 minutes.

12. Hysteria:

This is a neurological condition involving psychological syndromes caus-ed by mental depression and mental distress due to the stagnation of qi.

Differential diagnosis: Patients with stagnation of liver qi may suffer from mental depression, emotional distress, frequent sighing, distension and pain in chest and flank, sense of obstruction in throat and difficulty in swallowing, white and greasy tongue coating, and wiry and rolling pulse. Patients with mental distress due to worry may suffer from mental confusion and unsteadiness, crying, pale tongue with white coating, and wiry and thready pulse. And patients with deficiency of Yin and excessive Yang may suffer from vertigo, insomnia, annoyance or emission of semen, soreness of waist, irregular menstruation, red tongue, and wiry, thready and rapid pulse. Neurasthenia and menopausal syndrome recognized by modern medicine may be treated by the following methods.

Treatment:

(1) Foot massage: The massage may be applied to head 1, pituitary gland 4,

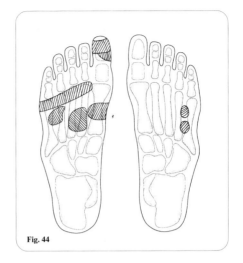

Fig. 44

spleen 34, stomach 15, liver 18, kidney 22, heart 33 and lung 14 reflecting areas (Fig. 44).

(2) Foot acupuncture:

1) Meridianal acupoints: Bilateral Xingjian (LR 2) or Taichong (LR 3) are used for liver qi stagnation by a lifting, thrusting and twisting stimulation for 10 times, with 5-minute intervals between, and the needles retained for 20 minutes.

2) Extra acupoints: At Neizhiyin (EX-F 20) and Nuxi (EX-F 6) acupoints, a strong reducing technique is applied and the needles are retained for 20 minutes.

3) Foot acupoints: At Epilepsy (FA-M 4) and Anmian (FA-P 2) acupoints, a moderate twisting stimulation is applied and the needles are retained for 20 minutes, and Liver (FA-P 9) acupoint is used for liver qi stagnation.

13. Epilepsy:

This is a neurological condition causing convulsions. It is divided into primary and secondary types in modern medicine.

Differential diagnosis: Patients suffering from severe epilepsy may experience sudden falls, loss of consciousness, lockjaw, spitting of white foam from the mouth, opisthotonus, convulsions, and stiff neck and screaming during the attack and soreness, pain and weakness of body after the attack. Patients of the deficient type may suffer from repeated attacks of convulsions, cold sweats and dyspnea during the attack, and lassitude, vertigo, heart palpitations, loss of appetite, soreness and weakness of waist and knees, and the impairment of mental activity after the attack.

Treatment:

(1) Foot massage:

The massage can be applied to head 1, brain stem and cerebellum 3, kidney 22, heart 33 and spleen 34 reflecting areas (Fig. 45).

(2) Foot acupuncture:

1) Meridianal acupoints: At Lidui (ST 45), Xingjian (LR 2), Kunlun (BL 60), Pucan (BL 61), Jinmen (BL 63), Shugu (BL 65) and Jiexi (ST 41) acupoints, the reducing technique is applied; Yongquan (KI 1)

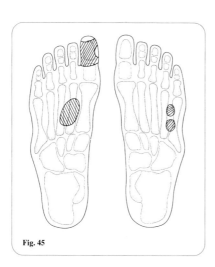

is added for patients with continuous loss of consciousness and coma, and moxibustion is applied before the attack.

2) Extra acupoints: Zu-xin (EX-F 18) and Lin-eiting (FA-F 21) acup-oints are used, a strong reducing technique is applied to the excessive type and the reinforcing technique is applied to the deficient type, and

Fig. 45

90

the needles are retained for 20 minutes. Moxibustion after acupuncture is applied to the deficient type.

3) Foot acupoints: At Epilepsy (FA-M 4), Heart (FA-P 5) and Spleen (FA-P 10) acupoints, a moderate twisting stimulation is applied and the needles are retained for 20 minutes.

14. Psychosis:

This is a mental condition including confusion and disturbance of speech and behavior patterns.

Differential diagnosis: Patients with stagnation of phlegm may suffer from apathy, mental dullness, incoherent speech, delusions, strange behavior, poor personal hygiene, greasy tongue coating, and wiry and rolling pulse. Patients with heart and spleen deficiency may suffer from forgetfulness, heart palpitations, chest distress, sadness, weakness, pale tongue, and thready and weak pulse. Maniac patients afflicted by the upward disturbance of phlegm-fire may suffer from impetuosity, headache, insomnia, fierce staring and injuring others, insomnia, red tongue with yellow and greasy coating, and wiry, large, rolling and rapid pulse. And maniac patients suffering from depletion of Yin and excessive fire may experience fatigue, fright, endless talking, restlessness, insomnia, pathological leanness, flushed face, red tongue, and thready and rapid pulse. Patients diagnosed with schizophrenia, manic psychosis, depressive psychosis and menopausal psychosis by modern medicine can be treated by the following methods.

Treatment:

(1) Foot massage:

The massage can be applied to head 1, pituitary gland 4, thyroid gland 12, spleen 34, heart 33, liver 18 and kidney 22 reflecting areas (Fig. 46).

(2) Foot acupuncture:

1) Meridianal acupoints: At Pucan (BL 61), Zutonggu (BL 66), Shangqiu (SP 5), Zhaohai (KI 6) and Shenmai (BL 62) acupoints, a

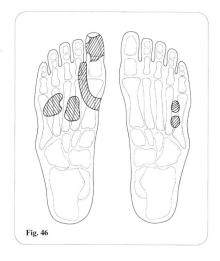

Fig. 46

strong reducing technique is applied for stagnation of phlegm and upward disturbance of phlegm-fire, and a moderate balanced reinforce-reducing technique is applied for heart and spleen deficiency and depletion of Yin by excessive fire. Moxibustion after acupuncture may be applied for heart and spleen deficiency.

2) Extra acupoint: The strong reducing stimulation is applied at Nuxi (EX-F 6) acupoint and the needle is retained for 20 minutes.

3) Foot acupoints: At Anmian (FA-P 2), Kidney (FA-P 14), Liver (FA-P 9) and Heart (FA-P 5) acupoints, a moderate twisting stimulation is applied and the needles are retained for 20 minutes.

15. Stomachache:

This is a condition of pain in the epigastric region.

Differential diagnosis: Patients with stomachache caused by cold pathogens may suffer from severe stomach pain, no thirst or preference for hot drinks, vomiting of saliva or clear fluid, white tongue coating, and wiry and slow pulse. Patients with food stagnation may suffer from distension and pain in stomach, anorexia, nausea, relief of stomachache after vomiting, discharge of foul stool and wind from bowel, thick and greasy tongue coating, and wiry and rolling pulse. Patients with liver qi stagnation may suffer from distension and pain in epigastric region radiated to bilateral flanks and aggravated by stimulation, chest distress, loss of appetite, regurgitation of sour fluid, thin and white tongue coating, and wiry pulse. And patients with blood stasis may suffer from fixed pricking pain in stomach aggravated after eating, hematemesis, discharge of dark stool, dark purple tongue, and thready and uneven pulse. Acute and chronic gastritis, gastric and duodenal peptic ulcer, gastric colic, gastrointestinal neurosis and stomachache without organic lesion recognized by modern medicine can be treated by the following methods.

Treatment:

(1) Foot massage:

The massage can be applied to stomach 15, duodenum 16, spleen 34, lymph nodes (abdomen, 40) and coeliac plexus 20 reflecting areas (Fig. 47).

(2) Foot acupuncture:

1) Meridianal acupoints: At Gongsun (SP 4), Dadu (SP 2), Taibai (SP 3), Xingjian (LR 2) and Zhiyin (BL 67) acupoints, a reducing technique is applied and the needles are retained for 20 minutes, and moxibustion after acupuncture may be applied to patients with stomachache caused by cold pathogens.

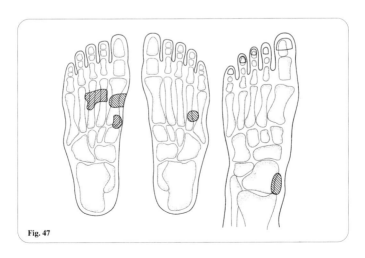

Fig. 47

2) Foot acupoints: At Stomach (FA-P 8), Stomach and intestine (FA-D 7), Spleen (FA-P 10) and small intestine (FA-P 11) acupoints, a moderate twisting stimulation is applied and the needles are retained for 20 minutes, and moxibustion after acupuncture may be applied to patients with stomachache caused by cold pathogens.

16. Ptosis of stomach:
A condition in which the stomach is at an abnormally low position. Differential diagnosis: Patients with liver qi stagnation may suffer from impetuosity, anger, distension and pain in bilateral flanks, mental depression, aggravation of symptoms after emotional disturbance, pale tongue with white or yellow and thin coating, and wiry pulse. And patients with deficiency of qi and blood may suffer from general fatigue and weakness, poor appetite, vomiting without vomitus, hiccup, pale tongue with white coating, and thready and weak pulse.
Treatment:
(1) Foot massage:
The massage is applied to stomach 15, kidney 22, duodenum 16, small intestine 25, ascending colon 28, transverse colon 29 and descending colon 30 reflecting areas (Fig. 48).

(2) Foot acupuncture:
1) Meridianal acupoints: At Chongyang (ST 42), Shangqiu (SP 5), Neiting (ST 44), and Yinbai (SP 1) acupoints, a reinforcing technique is applied to patients with qi and blood deficiency, and Taichong

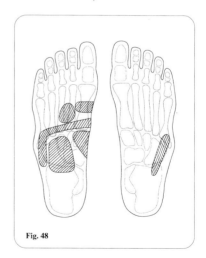

Fig. 48

94

(LR 3) is added to above acupoints and a reducing technique is applied to patients with liver qi stagnation and the needles are retained for 20 minutes.

2) Foot acupoints: At Stomach (FA-P 8), Spleen (FA-P 10) and Stomach and intestine (FA-D 7) acupoints, a moderate twisting stimulation is applied and the needles are retained for 20 minutes, Liver (FA-P 9) acupoint is added for patients with liver qi stagnation, and moxibustion after acupuncture is applied to patients with qi and blood deficiency.

17. Hiccups:

Hiccups are a condition in which gas (stomach qi) is automatically squeezed out of the throat by diaphragm spasms.

Differential diagnosis: Patients with cold pathogens in the stomach may suffer from slow hiccups, discomfort of upper abdomen relieved by heat and exacerbated by cold, reduction of appetite, no thirst, pale tongue with white and moist coating, and slow and moderate pulse. Patients with heat pathogens in the stomach may suffer from quick hiccups, foul breath, preference for cold drinks, flushed face, red tongue with yellow coating, and rolling and rapid pulse. Patients with qi stagnation may suffer from hiccups induced by mental depression or anger, fullness and distension of chest and flank, vertigo, pale tongue with thin and greasy coating, and wiry and rolling pulse. And patients with vital energy deficiency may suffer from hiccups, cold limbs, reduction of appetite, weakness, pale tongue with white and thin coating, and thready and weak pulse. Hiccups caused by gastrointestinal neurosis, gastritis, dilatation of stomach, peptic ulcer of stomach, late stage of liver cirrhosis, cerebrovascular diseases, uremia and severe infection recognized by modern medicine may be treated by the following methods.

Treatment:

Foot massage: The massage can be applied to coeliac plexus 20, parathyroid gland 13, diaphragm 44, stomach 15, kidney 22 and duodenum 16 reflecting areas (Fig. 49).

18. Flank pain:
Patients may have pain in one or both flanks.
Differential diagnosis: Patients with liver stagnation may suffer from pain in flank of left or right side alleviated after relief from mental depression but aggravated by emotional distress, annoyance, anger, impairment of

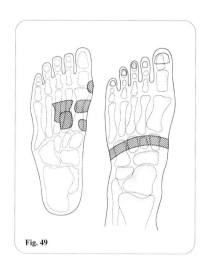

Fig. 49

sleep, thin tongue coating, and wiry pulse. Patients with damp-heat pathogens may suffer from pain in flank of right side, bitter taste in mouth, chest distress, nausea, vomiting, red or yellow eyes, jaundice, discharge of dark yellow urine, yellow and greasy tongue coating, and wiry pulse. Patients with blood stasis may suffer from fixed pain in flank worse at night with history of external trauma, mass in abdomen, dark purple tongue, and deep and uneven pulse. And patients with Yin deficiency may suffer from dull pain in flank without fixed location and aggravated by physical exertion, sallow complexion, hot sensation in heart, vertigo, red tongue with scanty coating, and thready and rapid pulse. Acute and chronic diseases of the liver, gallbladder, pleura and intercostal neuralgia recognized by modern medicine may be treated by the following methods.
Treatment:
(1) Foot massage:
The massage is applied to liver 18, gallbladder 19, spleen 34, stomach 15 and coeliac plexus 20 reflecting areas (Fig. 50).
(2) Foot acupuncture:

At Xingjian (LR 2), Taichong (LR 3), Qiuxu (GB 40), Zulinqi (GB 41) and Zuqiaoyin (BL 67) acupoints, a reducing technique is applied to patients with liver qi stagnation and blood stasis and a balanced reinforcereducing technique is applied to patients with Yin deficiency.

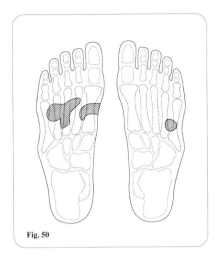

Fig. 50

19. Diarrhea:

Diarrhea is a condition of increased bowel movements and thin and loose stool.

Differential diagnosis: Patients with cold and damp pathogens may suffer from discharge of thin or watery stool, abdominal pain, increased intestinal gurgling sound, reduction of appetite, thin and white or white and greasy tongue coating, and soft and moderate pulse. Patients with damp-heat pathogens may suffer from abdominal pain, diarrhea with urgent discharge of yellow or brown foul stool and tenesmus, hot sensation in anus, yellow and greasy tongue coating, and soft and rapid or rolling and rapid pulse. Patients with food stagnation may suffer from abdominal pain, increased intestinal gurgling sound, diarrhea with discharge of sour and foul stool, reduction of abdominal pain after bowel movement, dirty or thick and greasy tongue coating, and rolling pulse. Patients with an attack of liver qi to spleen may suffer from distress in chest and flank, reduction of appetite, mental depression and nervousness, abdominal pain, diarrhea, pink tongue, and wiry pulse. Patients with deficiency and weakness of spleen and stomach may suffer from diarrhea after intake of greasy food, reduction of appetite, sallow complexion, weakness of limbs, increased bowel movements, pale tongue with white coating, and thready and weak pulse. And patients with deficiency of kidney Yang may suffer from diarrhea in the early morning and after intestinal gurgling sound, abdominal pain relievable after bowel movement, white tongue coating, and deep and thready pulse.

Treatment:

(I) Foot massage:

The massage may be applied to spleen 34, stomach 15, liver 18, kidney 22, ascending, transverse and descending colon 28, 29 and 30 reflecting areas (Fig. 51).

(2) Foot acupuncture:

1) Meridianal acupoints: At Jiexi (ST 41), Neiting (ST 44), Lidui (ST 45), Rangu (KI 2), Yinbai (SP 1), Dadu (SP 2), Gongsun (SP 4) and Shangqiu (SP 5) acupoints, a reinforcing technique is applied to patients with kidney Yang deficiency and a reducing technique is applied to patients of other types, and the needles are retained for 20 minutes, and moxibustion after acupuncture may be applied to patients with cold and damp pathogens or kidney Yang deficiency.

2) Extra acupoints: At Yinyang (EX-F 5) and Ranhou (EX-F 12) the reinforcing technique is applied to patients with deficiency of spleen and stomach and kidney Yang deficiency, and the reducing tech-

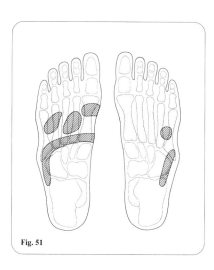

Fig. 51

98

nique is applied to patients of other types; the needles are retained for 20 minutes.

3) Foot acupoints: At Stomach and intestine (FA-D 7), Colon (FA-P 13), Small intestine (FA-P 11) and Spleen (FA-P 10) acupoints, a moderate twisting stimulation is applied and the needles are retained for 20 minutes.

20. Bacillary dysentery:

This is an infectious disease of the intestines caused by dysentery bacilli with chill, fever, abdominal pain, nausea, vomiting, and diarrhea with discharge of watery stool many times in a day at the beginning, and later with passage of pus and bloody stool, scanty in amount, sticky in nature, and pink or fresh red in color. If the disease is not effectively cured at the early stage, the patient may suffer from fever, dizziness, fatigue, high fever, lassitude, restlessness, pale complexion, cold limbs, hypotension, coma, collapse, cyanosis, and respiratory failure.

Treatment:

(1) Foot massage:

The massage may be applied to lymph nodes (upper body, 39),

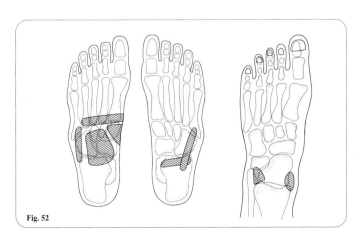

Fig. 52

lymph nodes (abdomen, 40), small intestine 25, ascending, transverse and descending colon 28, 29 and 30 and rectum 31 reflecting areas (Fig. 52).

(2) Foot acupuncture:

1) Meridianal acupoints: At Gongsun (SP 4), Shugu (BL 65), Neiting (ST 44), Taibai (SP 3) and Shangqiu (SP 5) acupoints, a reducing technique is applied to the acute patient, and a reinforcing technique or moxibustion after acupuncture is applied to the patient with chronic diarrhea; the needles are retained for 20 minutes and Yongquan (KI 1) may be added for patients with high fever and hypotension.

2) Foot acupoints: At Small intestine (FA-P 11) and Colon (FA-P 13) acupoints, a moderate twisting stimulation is applied and the needles are retained for 20 minutes.

(3) External application of drugs:

1) A proper amount of garlic is pounded to prepare a paste for application over the central area of both soles.

2) The powder of Wuzhuyu (evodia fruit) 6 gm is mixed with vinegar to prepare a paste for application into the umbilicus and over bilateral Yongquan (KI 1) acupoints.

21. Constipation:

In patients with constipation, the stool is dry and hard, defecation is difficult, and the time between bowel movements is prolonged. Differential diagnosis: Patients with heat pathogens may suffer from constipation with dry stool passed once after several days, abdominal pain, hot body and flushed face. Patients with cold pathogens may suffer from difficult bowel movement, cold and pain in abdomen, and cold limbs. Patients with qi stagnation may suffer from frequent belching, difficult bowel movement, and distension and pain in abdomen. Patients with qi deficiency may suffer from difficult defecation, and fatigue after bowel movement. Patients with blood deficiency may suffer from difficult defecation with dry stool, sallow complexion, dizziness and heart palpitations. Patients with Yin deficiency may suffer from difficult defecation with dry stool, dryness in mouth and throat, body leanness, flushed cheeks, and low tidal fever in the afternoon. And patients with Yang deficiency may suffer from difficult bowel movement, cold limbs, preference for hot and aversion to cold.

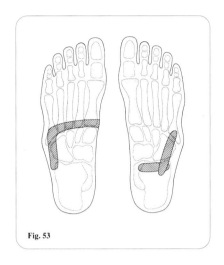

Fig. 53

Treatment:

(1) Foot massage:

The massage may be applied to rectum 31, anus 32, ascending, transverse and descending colon 28, 29 and 30 reflecting areas (Fig. 53).

(3) Foot acupuncture:

Meridianal acupoints: At Jiexi (ST 41), Neiting (ST 44), Gongsun (SP 4), Shangqiu (SP 5) and Rangu (KI 2) acupoints, a strong reducing technique is applied to patients with cold or heat pathogens or with qi stagnation; a balanced reinforce-reducing technique is applied to patients with deficiency of Yang, Yin, qi or blood, the needles are retained for 20 minutes, and moxibustion after acupuncture may be applied to patients with cold pathogens or with deficiency of Yang, qi or blood.

22. Diabetes mellitus:

This is a metabolic and endocrinal condition with disturbance of

carbohydrate metabo-
lism due to functional
reduction of pancreatic
islets with increase of
appetite and profuse
discharge of urine, loss
of body weight, and
complications of
hypertension, coronary
heart disease, cerebral
hemorrhage, cerebral
thrombosis, cerebral
embolism, and gan-
grene of limbs.

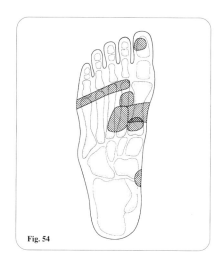

Fig. 54

Treatment:

(1) Foot massage:

The massage is applied to pancreas 17, pituitary gland 4, stomach
15, kidney 22, adrenal gland 21, lung 14 and urinary bladder 24
reflecting areas (Fig. 54).

(2) Foot acupuncture:

Meridianal acupoints: At Taixi (KI 3), Rangu (KI 2), Xingjian (LR 2),
Zhaohai (KI 6), Zhongfeng (LR 4), Yinbai (SP 1) and Shangqiu (SP 5)
acupoints, a balanced reinforce-reducing technique is applied and
the needles are retained for 20 minutes.

23. Vertigo:

The major symptoms of vertigo are blurred vision and dizziness.
Differential diagnosis: Patients with upward exacerbation of liver
Yang may suffer from tinnitus, distending pain in head aggravated
by anger, bitter taste in mouth, insomnia, dreaminess, red tongue
with yellow coating, and wiry pulse. Patients with qi and blood
deficiency may suffer from heart palpitations, chest distress,
insomnia, general malaise, pale complexion and aggravation of

symptoms when fatigued, pale tongue, and thready and weak pulse. Patients with kidney essence deficiency may suffer from poor memory, soreness of waist, weakness of lower limbs, emission of semen, and tinnitus. Patients with Yang deficiency may suffer from cold limbs, pale tongue, and deep pulse. Patients with Yin deficiency may suffer from hotness in palms and soles, annoyance, red tongue with scanty coating, and wiry pulse. And patients with turbid phlegm may suffer from heaviness of head, nausea, vomiting, chest distress, poor appetite, fatigue, sleepiness, white and greasy tongue coating, and soft and rolling pulse. Vertigo in patients with diseases of the inner ear, cerebral arteriosclerosis, hypertension, anemia, neurasthenia and other brain diseases recognized by modern medicine may be treated by the following methods.

Treatment:

(1) Foot massage:

The massage may be applied to head 1, brain stem and cerebellum 3 pituitary gland 4 balance organ (labyrinth, 42), frontal sinus 2 and kidney 22 reflecting areas (Fig. 55).

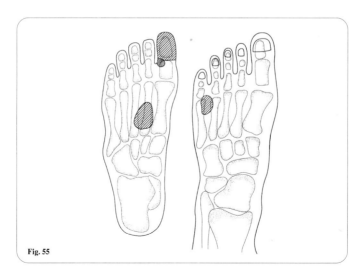

Fig. 55

(2) Foot acupuncture:

1) Meridianal acupoints: At Kunlun (BL 60), Shenmai (BL 62), Xingjian (LR 2), Taichong (LR 3) and Jiexi (ST 41) acupoints a balanced reinforce-reducing technique is applied, the needles are retained for 20 minutes, and moxibustion af ter acupuncture may be applied to patients with kidney essence deficiency or deficiency of qi and blood or kidney Yang.

2) Extra acupoints: At Xiaozhijian (tip of little toe), Zuxin (EX-F 18) and Dazhi Jumao (EX-F 14) acupoints, a reducing technique is applied to patients with exacerbation of liver Yang or turbid phlegm; and a reinforcing technique is applied to patients with deficiency of qi, blood, kidney essence, Yang or Yin, and the needles are retained for 20 minutes.

3) Foot acupoints: At Kidney (FA-P 14) and Vertigo (FA-M 1) acupoints, a moderate twisting stimulation is applied and the needles are retained for 20 minutes. Liver (FA-P 9) acupoint is added for patients with exacerbation of liver Yang, and Lung (FA- P 6) and Spleen (FA-P 10) acupoints are added for patients with turbid phlegm. Moxibustion after acupuncture may be applied to patients with turbid phlegm, deficiency of qi and blood or deficiency of kidney essence or Yang.

(3) External application of drugs:

For patients with exacerbation of liver Yang, the powder of Wuzhuyu (evodia trait, mixed with bile) 100 gm, Longdancao (gentian root) 50 gm, Liuhuang (sulfur) 20 gm, Zhusha (cinnabar) 15 gm and Mingfan (alum) 30 gm are mixed with the juice of Xiaojigen (root of field thistle) to prepare a paste for application into umbilicus and bilateral Yongquan (KI 1) acupoints, 10-15 gm at each acupoint. The application is changed every other day and continued for one month and the therapeutic effect may appear after the application of this drug for 7 to 10 days. Vertigo may be relieved after treatment over 2 to 3 months.

(4) Foot bath:

A warm decoction of Xiakucao (selfheal spike) 30 gm, Gouteng (uncaria stem) 20 gm, Sangye (mulberry leaf) 15 gm and Juhua (chrysanthemum) 20 gm is used to wash both feet for 10 to 15 minutes, one or two times a day. The treatment is continued for 10 to 15 days as a therapeutic course.

24. Impotence:

Impotence is a condition in which the penis is unable to gain full erection. Sexual disabilities due to defects or chronic inflammation of male reproductive organs, organic lesions of endocrinal glands, or tumor of central nervous system can be treated by the following methods.

Treatment:

Foot massage:

The massage is applied to reproductive gland 36, penis 51, inguinal groove 49, pituitary gland 4, prostate gland 50, adrenal gland 21 and kidney 22 reflecting areas (Fig. 56).

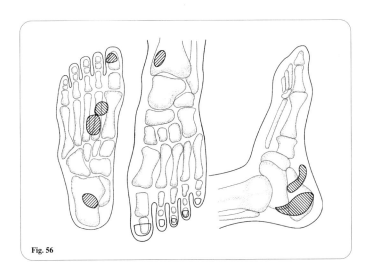

Fig. 56

25. Emission of semen:

This is a spontaneous discharge of semen without sexual activity, usually once every 1-2 or 3-4 days.

Differential diagnosis: Patients with Yin deficiency may suffer from emission of semen with dreams of sexual activity, dizziness, tinnitus, unstable sleep, lassitude, weakness of body, red tip of tongue, and thready and rapid pulse. Patients with poor kidney function may suffer from repeated emission of semen, dizziness, vertigo, soreness of waist, sallow complexion, aversion to cold, cold limbs, pale tongue with white and thin coating, and deep, thready and weak pulse. And patients with damp-heat pathogens may suffer from frequent emission, discharge of small amounts of semen during urination of hot and turbid urine, annoyance, unstable sleep, dryness and bitter taste in mouth, thirst without desire to drink much water, yellow and greasy tongue coating, and soft and rapid pulse. The emission of semen in sexual neurotics, acute and chronic inflammation of prostate gland, urethra, seminal vesicle, testis, epididymis or prepuce can be treated by the following methods.

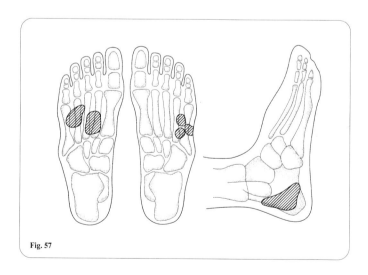

Fig. 57

106

Treatment:

(1) Foot massage:

The massage is applied to kidney 22, liver 18, spleen 34, stomach 15, heart 33 and reproductive gland 36 reflecting areas (Fig. 57).

(2) Foot acupuncture:

1) Meridianal acupoints: At Gongsun (SP 4), Zhiyin (BL 67), Rangu (KI 2), Taixi (KI 3) and Zhongfeng (LR 4) acupoints, a reinforcing technique is applied to patients with deficiency of Yin and poor storage function of kidney, a reducing technique is applied to patients with damp-heat pathogens and the needles are retained for 20 minutes; and moxibustion after acupuncture may be applied to patients with poor storage function of kidney.

2) Extra acupoint: At Quchi (EX-F 10) acupoint, a balanced reinforce-reducing technique is applied and the needle is retained for 20 minutes.

(3) Foot bath:

Warm water of 50-60 degrees centigrade in a wood or enamal basin is used to soak and wash both feet for 8 to 10 minutes once each night before going to bed with a calm mind.

26. Stranguria:

Stranguria patients may suffer from cramps in lower abdomen and frequent and urgent urination with pain in urethra and sensation of unfinished urination.

Differential diagnosis: Patients with stranguria of the heat type may suffer from dysuria with frequent discharge of small amount of dark and turbid urine and burning pain in urethra, distending and straining sensation in lower abdomen, and red tongue with yellow and greasy coating. Patients with stones in the urinary tract may suffer from distending pain in lower abdomen and urinary tract, temporary blockage of urination relievable by a change of posture, sand and blood in dark urine, white or yellow and greasy tongue coating, and wiry and rapid pulse, and colic in abdomen or waist in patients with stones in upper and middle urinary tract, severe pain in abdomen. Patients with hematuria may suffer from frequent and urgent urination of bloody urine, pricking pain in urethra, mild pain in lower abdomen, yellow and greasy tongue coating or red tongue with scanty coating, and thready and rapid pulse. Patients with qi disturbance may suffer from distending pain on both sides of lower abdomen and perineal region, feeble urination with repeated discharge of urine in drops, shallow breath, no desire to speak, pale tongue, and thready and weak pulse. And patients with chyluria may suffer from difficult discharge of turbid urine with oily supernatant and sediment of flocculi, clots, blood streaks and blood clots, dryness in mouth, white and greasy tongue coating, and soft and rapid pulse. Patients with the above symptoms caused by acute and chronic infection, stones or tuberculosis of urinary tract, acute or chronic prostatitis and chyluria may be treated by the following methods.

Treatment:

(1) Foot massage:

The massage is applied to kidney 22, urinary bladder 24, ureter 23, parathyroid gland 13, lymph nodes (abdomen, 40), stomach 15, lung 14 and prostate gland 50 reflecting areas (Fig. 58).

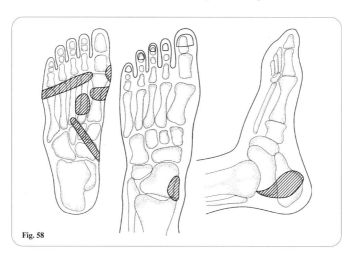

Fig. 58

(2) Foot acupuncture:

I) Meridianal acupoints: The moderate stimulation is applied at bilateral Taixi (KI 3) acupoints for pain due to stones in urethra and the needles are retained for 30 to 90 minutes.

2) Foot acupoints:

At Urinary bladder (FA-P 15), Kidney (FA-P 14) and Bed-wetting (FA-P 21) acupoints, a moderate twisting stimulation is applied and the needles retained for 20 minutes.

(3) External application of drugs:

One handful of fresh lettuce and Huangbai (Phellodendron bark) 10 gm are pounded together to prepare a paste for application over Yongquan (KI 1) acupoints on both sides to treat hematuria.

27. Bi-syndrome:

Bi-syndrome is caused by the attack of wind, cold, heat and damp pathogens blocking the meridians, with soreness and pain in muscles, tendons, bones and joints, numbness and heaviness of limbs, difficulty in moving, and swelling and heat in joints.

Differential diagnosis: Patients with wandering Bi-syndrome may suffer from wandering pain without a fixed location, inflexible movement of limbs, thin and white tongue coating, and floating pulse. Patients with painful Bi-syndrome may suffer from cold and severe pain in muscles and limb joints aggravated by cold and alleviated by heat, white tongue coating, and wiry and tense pulse. Patients with fixed Bi-syndrome may suffer from soreness, pain and heaviness of joints with fixed location aggravated by rainy, windy and cold weather, inflexible limbs, numbness of skin and muscles, white and greasy tongue coating, and soft and moderate pulse. And patients with heat Bi-syndrome may suffer from soreness, pain, swelling and limitation of limb-joint movement, fever not relieved by sweating, yellow, thick and greasy tongue coating, and soft and rapid pulse. Rheumatic fever, rheumatic arthritis and myofibrositis recognized by modern medicine can be treated by the following methods.

Treatment:

(1) Foot massage:

The massage is applied to spleen 34, stomach 15, kidney 22, lung 14, lymph nodes (upper body, 39), lymph nodes (abdomen, 40), lymph nodes (chest, 41), adrenal gland 21 and other correspondent reflecting areas of lesions on the limbs (Fig. 59).

(2) Foot acupuncture:

1) Meridianal acupoints: At Jiexi (ST 41), Kunlun (BL 60), Pucan (BL 61), Shenmai (BL 62), Jinmen (BL 63) and Shangqiu (SP 5) acupoints, a reducing technique is applied and the needles are retained for 20 minutes, and moxibustion after acupuncture may be applied to patients with Bi-syndrome, except those of the heat type.

2) Extra acupoints: At Xiakunlun (EX-F 3) and Qiduan (EX-F 23) acupoints, a balanced reinforce-reducing technique is applied and the needles are retained for 20 minutes, and moxibustion after acupuncture may be applied to Bi-syndrome patients except those of the heat type.

(3) External application of drugs:

1) The powder of Wuzhuyu (evodia fruit) 31 gm and fresh ginger 3 gm is fried with alcohol and wrapped in a bag for application over

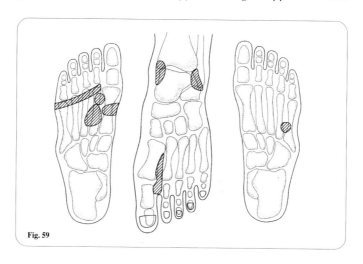

Fig. 59

the central area of both soles to relieve pain in lower limbs.

2) Wuzhuyu (evodia fruit) 16 gm and one bulb of garlic are pounded to prepare a paste for application over the central area of both soles to treat wandering, painful, and fixed Bi-syndrome.

28. Periarthritis of shoulder:

This is an aseptic inflammation of soft tissues around the shoulder joint with pain difficult to locate but radiated to upper arm and forearm and exacerbated by arm movement. Chronic patients may have muscular atrophy and stiffness of shoulder joint.

Differential diagnosis: Patients with deficiency of qi and blood may suffer from fatigue, weakness, poor appetite, aggravation of symptoms when tired, numbness of involved limb, pale tongue with white coating, and thready and weak pulse. Patients with this condition caused by cold and damp pathogens may suffer from chills, aversion to cold, symptoms relieved by heat, tendency to press and knead local lesion, cool sensation in involved limb, pale tongue with white coating, and deep pulse. And patients with trauma of local soft tissues may suffer from local pain with aversion to pressing the lesion and with a history of injury, petechiae on tongue, and wiry or uneven pulse.

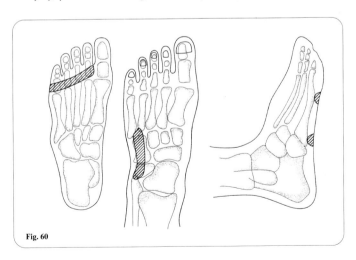

Fig. 60

Treatment:

(1) Foot massage:

The massage is applied to shoulder 10, elbow joint 60 and trapezius muscle 11 reflecting areas (Fig. 60).

(2) Foot acupuncture:

1) Meridianal acupoints: At Kunlun (BL 60), Jinggu (BL 64), Lidui (ST 45) and Qiuxu (GB 40) acupoints, a reinforcing technique is applied to patients with qi and blood deficiency and a strong reducing technique is applied to patients with cold and damp pathogens or external trauma, the needles are retained for 20 minutes.

2) Foot acupoint: At Ischium 1 (FA-P 18) acupoints, a moderate twisting stimulation is applied and the needle is retained for 20 minutes, and moxibustion after acupuncture is applied to patients with qi and blood deficiency.

29. Lumbago:

Lumbago patients may have pain in one or both sides of the waist. Differential diagnosis: Patients with cold and damp pathogens may suffer from cold pain and heaviness in the waist, more severe on cloudy and rainy days but alleviated or relieved by heat, limitation of waist movement, white and greasy tongue coating, and slow and moderate pulse. Patients with blood stasis may suffer from severe pricking pain in a fixed location of the waist, more severe when pressed and at night but reduced during the day, limited waist movement in mild cases and great difficulty in severe cases, dark purple tongue, and uneven pulse. Patients with kidney deficiency may suffer from soreness, weakness and pain of waist and legs, and aggravation of local pain after long standing or fatigue. Patients with kidney Yang deficiency may have a pale complexion, aversion to cold, and cold limbs; and patients with Yin kidney deficiency may have flushed face, insomnia, dryness in mouth and throat, hotness in palms and soles, red tongue, and wiry, thready and rapid pulse. Lumbago in patients with kidney diseases, rheumatic diseases, rheumatoid diseases, strain, trauma and inflammation of muscles and bones in waist may be treated by the following methods.

Treatment:

(1) Foot massage:

The massage is applied to kidney 22, lumbar spine 55, ureter 23 and urinary bladder 24 reflecting areas (Fig. 61).

(2) Foot acupuncture:

1) Meridianal acupoints: At Jiexi (ST 41), Yongquan (KI 1), Taixi (KI 3), Dazhong (KI 4) and Taichong (LR 3) acupoints, a reducing technique is applied for patients with cold and damp pathogens or blood stasis, and a reinforcing technique is applied to patients with kidney deficiency. Moxibustion after acupuncture is applied to patients with cold and damp pathogens and kidney deficiency, and Shugu (BL 65) is added for lumbago due to blood stasis. During retention of needles, the patient is helped to do sit-ups and a gentle rotation and forward and backward motion of the waist is performed after removal of needles.

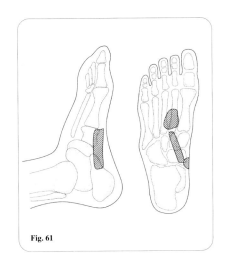

Fig. 61

2) Extra acupoints: At Xiakunlun (EX-F 3) and Quanshengzu (EX-F 7) acupoints, a reducing technique is applied to patients with cold and damp pathogens or blood stasis, and a reinforcing technique is applied to patients with deficiency of kidney Yang or kidney Yin. The needles are retained for 20 minutes and moxibustion after acupuncture is applied to patients with cold and damp pathogens or kidney Yang deficiency.

3) Foot acupoints: At Lumbago (FA-D 4), Waist and leg (FA-D 9), Kidney (FA-P 14) and Ischium 1 (FA-P 18) acupoints, a moderate twisting stimulation is applied and the needles are retained for 20 minutes. Moxibustion after acupuncture is applied to patients with cold and damp pathogens or kidney Yang deficiency.

30. Sciatic neuralgia:

The pain caused by this condition is distributed along the sciatic nerve.

Differential diagnosis: Patients with cold and damp pathogens may suffer from heaviness of body, stiffness, soreness and pain of waist and leg, numbness of skin and muscles on lateral side of leg, preference for warmth and aversion to cold, white and greasy tongue coating, and deep pulse. Patients with blood stagnation may suffer from pricking pain and limitation of waist movement with history of trauma, aggravation of pain at night, dark purple tongue, and uneven pulse. And patients with vital energy deficiency may suffer repeated attacks of severe pain when fatigued but relieved after rest, weakness of waist and leg, sallow complexion, and deep and thready pulse. The symptoms of neuralgia sciatica caused by prolapse of lumbar intervertebral disc, piriform muscle syndrome, diseases of iliosacral joint, arthritis of hip joint, adnexitis, spondylitis, intraspinal tumor and muscular sprain of waist recognized by modern medicine may be treated by the following methods.

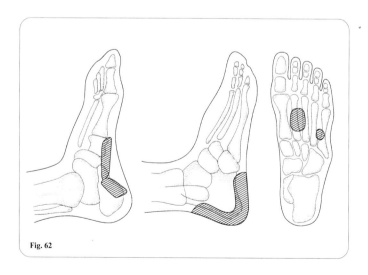

Fig. 62

Treatment:

(1) Foot massage:

The massage is applied to sciatic nerve 58, lumbar spine 55, sacrum 56, knee 35, kidney 22 and spleen 34 reflecting areas (Fig. 62).

(2) Foot acupuncture:

1) Meridianal acupoints: At Kunlun (BL 60), Pucan (BL 61), Shenmai (BL 62), Jinmen (BL 63) and Shugu (BL 65) acupoints, a reducing technique is applied to patients with cold and damp pathogens or blood stagnation, and a reinforcing technique is applied to patients with vital energy deficiency. The needles are retained for 20 minutes and moxibustion after acupuncture is applied to patients with cold and damp pathogens or vital energy deficiency.

2) Foot acupoints: At Buttocks (FA-L 1), Waist and leg (FA-D 9), Ischium 1 (FA-P 18) and Ischium 2 (FA-D 5) acupoints a moderate twisting stimulation is applied and the needles are retained for 15 minutes.

31. Cervical spondylosis:

Patients may suffer from stiffness and continuous pain or pricking pain in neck, usually on one side of neck, and a clicking noices in the neck while rotating the head, caused by improper spleeping posture, attack of wind and cold pathogens, lifting or carrying heavy loads, or working at a desk for a long time.

Differential diagnosis: Patients of the nerve-root type may suffer from neck pain, shoulder and occipital region stiffness and limitation of neck movement, radiating pain to shoulder and arm on one side, cold and numbness in one arm, and difficulty in lifting. Patients of the vertebral artery type may suffer from pain in neck, shoulder and occipital region, dizziness, nausea, vomiting, tinnitus and blurred vision which may be induced or aggravated by rotating the head or laterally over-extending the body. Patients of the spinal cord type may suffer from pain in neck and shoulders, numbness of limbs, weakness of both lower limbs, unsteady gait and disturbance of urination and defecation. Patients of the sympathetic nerve type may suffer from pain in occipital region, dizziness, migraine, dilatation of one pupil, reduction of skin temperature and polyhidrosis or ahidrosis on one arm and discomfort over precordial region. And patients of a mixed type may have the symptoms of two or more of above types.

Treatment:

(1) Foot massage:

The massage is applied to cervical spine 53, neck 7, elbow joint 60, trapezius muscle 11, frontal sinus 2, scapula 59 and shoulder 10 reflecting areas (Fig. 63).

(2) Foot acupuncture:

1) Meridianal acupoints: For nerve root type: At Kunlun (BL 60), Shugu (BL 65), Lidui (ST 45) and Qiuxu (GB 40) acupoints, a reducing technique is applied and the needles are retained for 20 minutes. Moxibustion after acupuncture may also be applied.

2) For vertebral artery and sympathetic nerve types: At Zutonggu

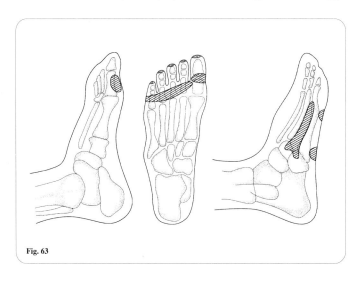

Fig. 63

(BL 66), Zhiyin (BL 67), Zulinqi (GB 41), Jiexi (ST 41) and Jinggu (BL 64) acupoints, a balanced reinforce-reducing technique is applied and the needles are retained for 20 minutes. Moxibustion after acupuncture may also be applied.

32. Rheumatoid arthritis:

This is a disease affecting the entire body with lesions in the small peripheral joints. It is included in the Bi-syndrome of traditional Chinese medicine. The onset of this disease is insidious, with fatigue, poor appetite, low fever, irregular menstruation, numbness of hands and feet, and pricking pain as the prodromal symptoms. Patients may then have pain, stiffness, redness and swelling of the finger or toe joints which assume a fusiform shape, and thereafter other joints may be gradually involved, developing the same lesions together with irregular fever, anemia, mental depression, and quick pulse.

Treatment:

(1) Foot massage:

The massage is applied to thoracic spine 54, lumbar spine 55,

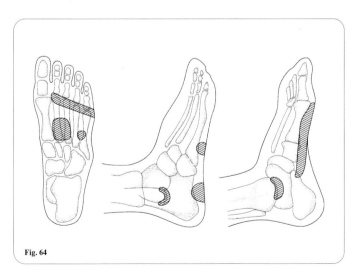

Fig. 64

kidney 22, spleen 34, lung 14, hip joint 38, knee 35 and elbow joint 60 reflecting areas (Fig. 64).

(2) Foot acupuncture:

Meridional acupoints: At Chongyang (ST 42), Xian'gu (ST 43), Qiuxu (GB 40), Zulinqi (GB 41), Diwuhui (GB 42), Pucan (BL 61), Jinmen (BL 63) and Shangqiu (SP 5) acupoints, a balanced reinforce-reducing technique is applied and the needles are retained for 30 minutes. Moxibustion after acupuncture is applied to patients not running a fever.

33. Poor memory:

Poor memory involves the reduction or loss of memory.

Differential diagnosis: Patients with spleen deficiency may suffer from mental fatigue, poor appetite, poor memory, pale tongue with white coating, and thready and weak pulse. Patients with kidney Yin deficiency may suffer from hotness in palms and soles, tidal fever in the afternoon, spontaneous sweating during sleep, red tongue, and thready and rapid pulse. Patients with Yang deficiency may suffer from aversion to cold, cold waist and knees, pale tongue with white and greasy coating, and deep and thready pulse. And patients with overfatigue of brain may suffer from mental trance, poor memory, general fatigue, insomnia, poor appetite, improvement of symptoms after rest, pale tongue with thin and white coating, and deep and thready pulse.

Treatment:

(1) Foot massage:

The massage is applied to head 1, brain stem and cerebellum 3, thyroid gland 12, adrenal gland 21, pituitary gland 4, spleen 34, kidney 22 and heart 33 reflecting areas (Fig. 65).

(2) Foot acupuncture:

Meridianal acupoints: At Kunlun (BL 60), Pucan (BL 61), Taixi (KI 3), Taibai (SP 3), Shangqiu (SP 5) and Rangu (KI 2) acupoints, a reinforcing technique is applied and the needles are retained for 20 minutes. Moxibustion after acupuncture may be applied to patients with spleen and Yang deficiency and mental fatigue.

(3) External application of drug:

An adequate amount of Suanzaoren (spiny jujube seeds) is pounded to prepare a paste for application over heart 33 reflecting area and affixed by a piece of adhesive plaster.

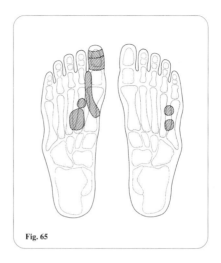

Fig. 65

34. Nephritis:

Nephritis, also called glomerulonephritis, is a disease of both kidneys caused by the invasion of external pathogens and dysfunction of lung, spleen and kidney. In acute nephritis, the patient may suffer from edema, hypertension, hematuria, proteinuria, chills and fever. In chronic nephritis the patient may suffer from edema, hypertension, weakness, and pale complexion.

Differential diagnosis: Patients with wind edema may suffer from edema of eyelids first which rapidly spreads to the limbs and entire body, soreness and heaviness of limbs, stanguria, red tongue, and floating, rolling and rapid pulse. Patients with edema caused by invasion of toxic pathogens from sores on the body surface may have furuncles or skin infection first, and then suffer from fever, edema, discharge of short streams of dark urine or hematuria, red tip and borders of tongue with thin and yellow coating, and rapid pulse. Patients with deficiency of spleen and kidney may suffer from general malaise, poor appetite, and small amount of protein and red blood cells in urine. Patients with deficiency of spleen and kidney qi may suffer from weakness, poor appetite, edema of feet, and small or medium amounts of protein in urine. Patients with deficiency of spleen and kidney Yang may suffer from severe edema of the whole body, cold body and limbs, poor appetite, oliguria and loose stool. And patients with deficiency of liver and kidney Yin may suffer from headache, dizziness, vertigo, anger, flushed face, chest distress, hypertension, red tongue, and wiry and thready pulse.

Treatment:

(1) Foot massage:

The massage is applied to kidney 22, ureter 23, urinary bladder 24, spleen 34, liver 18, lung 14, lymph nodes (abdomen, 40) and adrenal gland 21 reflecting areas (Fig. 66).

(2) Foot acupuncture:

1) Meridianal acupoints: At Jiexi (ST 41), Xian'gu (ST 43), Taibai (SP 3), Taixi (KI 3), Shuiquan (KI 5), Xingjian (LR 2) and Taichong (LR 3) acupoints, a reducing technique is applied to patients with wind edema or edema caused by invasion of toxic pathogens from external sores, and a reinforcing technique is applied to patients with deficiency of spleen and kidney or deficiency of liver and kidney

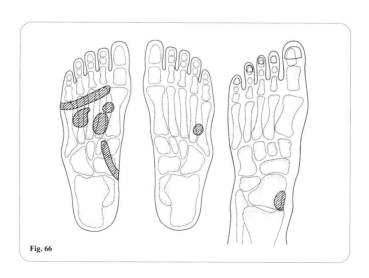

Fig. 66

120

Yang. The needles are retained for 20 minutes, and moxibustion after acupuncture may be applied to patients with wind edema, deficiency of spleen and kidney qi, or Yang deficiency.

2) Extra acupoint: A balanced reinforce-reducing technique is applied at Erzhishang (EX-F 16) acupoint and the needle is retained for 20 minutes.

3) Foot acupoints: At Kidney (FA-P 14), Spleen (FA-P 10) and Urinary bladder (FA-P 15) acupoints, a moderate twisting stimulation is applied and the needles are retained for 15 minutes. Liver (FA-P 9) acupoint may be added for patients with deficiency of liver and kidney Yin, and moxibustion after acupuncture may be applied to patients with wind edema, deficiency of spleen and kidney qi or deficiency of Yang.

(3) External application of drugs:

1) Acute and chronic nephritis: One bulb of garlic with purple skin peeled and Bimazi (castor bean) 60-70 grains with skin peeled are pounded to prepare a paste and divided into two portions for application over Yongquan (KI 1) acupoints on both soles for 7 days and affixed by a piece of transparent paper. If this is not effective, a new preparation may be applied for another 7 days.

2) Chronic nephritis: Shisuan (lycoris bulb) 2-3 bulbs and Bimazi (castor bean) 70 grains are pounded to prepare a paste for application over the central area of both soles and changed once every 12 hours for one week.

35. Vomiting:

The regurgitation of vomitus from stomach with or without vomiting noise is caused by the adverse ascent of stomach qi.

Differential diagnosis: Patients with vomiting caused by cold pathogens may have sudden vomiting with vomitus containing clear fluid and saliva, white tongue coating, and floating pulse. Patients whose conditions is caused by heat pathogens may have repeated vomiting with vomitus containing sour and bitter bile, thirst with desire to drink cold water, red tongue, and rapid pulse. Patients with vomiting caused by improper food may have vomiting with vomitus containing undigested food with relief of symptoms after vomiting, fullness and distension of upper abdomen, anorexia, foul stool, thick and greasy tongue coating, and rolling and forceful pulse. Patients with vomiting caused by stagnation of phlegm may suffer from distension of abdomen, vomiting with vomitus containing sputum, preference for hot drinks after vomiting, anorexia, dizziness, heart palpitations, pale tongue with white coating, and rolling and soft pulse. And patients with an attack of liver qi to the stomach may have vomiting after meals caused by emotional distress, relieved of symptoms after vomiting, fullness and distension or pain in chest and flank, annoyance and depression, red borders of tongue, and wiry pulse. Vomiting due to nerves, gastritis, spasms or obstruction of pylorus, cholecystitis, cerebrovascular accident and hepatic coma recognized by modern medicine may be treated by the following methods.

Treatment:

(1) Foot massage:

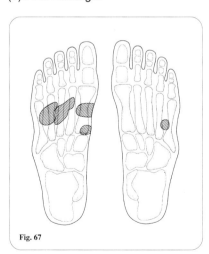

Fig. 67

The massage is applied to spleen 34, stomach 15, coeliac plexus 20, liver 18 and duodenum 16 reflecting areas (Fig. 67).

(2) Foot acupuncture:

1) Meridianal acupoints: At Qiuxu (GB 40), Pucan (BL 61), Zutonggu (BL 66), Yinbai (SP 1), Dadu (SP 2) and Taibai (SP 3) acupoints, a reducing technique is

applied and the needles are retained for 20 minutes. Moxibustion after acupuncture may be applied to patients with cold pathogens or phlegm stagnation.

2) Extra acupoint: A reducing technique is applied at Nuxi (EX-F 6) acupoint and the needle is retained for 20 minutes. Moxibustion after acupuncture may be applied to patients with cold pathogens or phlegm stagnation.

3) Foot acupoints: At Stomach (FA-P 8), Colon (FA-P 13), Small intestine (FA-P 11) and Spleen (FA-P 10) acupoints, a moderate twisting stimulation is applied with the needles not retained. Patients with vomiting caused by cold pathogens or phlegm stagnation may be treated with moxibustion after acupuncture with the needles retained for 20 minutes.

(3) External application of drugs:

1) After pig oil is smeared on the soles, a garlic paste is applied over the central area of both soles and wrapped with gauze.

2) The powder of alum and wheat flour in an adequate amount are mixed with vinegar or boiled water to prepare a paste for application over Yongquan (KI 1) acupoint and covered by a piece of sulfate paper and gauze.

(4) Foot bath:

For vomiting and diarrhea due to improper food, a warm decoction of 3000 ml in 40 degrees centigrade prepared by boiling pepper 20 gm, a handful of mung beans, Huanglian (Chinese goldthread rhizome) 120 gm and dry ginger 120 gm in water for 20 minutes is used for shower of chest and abdomen, and then for soaking and washing both feet for 30 to 60 minutes, one or two times a day.

36. Retention of urine:

In traditional Chinese medicine the retention of urine is called Longbi. Dysuria with urine discarged by drops is called Long and the complete obstruction of urination is called Bi.

Differential diagnosis: Patients with damp-heat pathogens in urinary bladder may suffer from retention of urine or frequent discharge of small amount of dark and hot urine, distension of lower abdomen, bitter taste and stickiness in mouth, red tongue with yellow, thick and greasy coating, and rapid pulse. Patients with accumulation of heat pathogens in lungs may suffer from retention of urine or dysuria with small amount of urine, dryness in throat, thirst with desire to drink water, yellow and thin tongue coating, and rapid pulse. Patients with liver qi stagnation may suffer from annoyance, anger, retention of urine or dysuria, distension of flank and costal region, red tongue with thin and yellow coating, and wiry pulse. And patients with kidney qi deficiency may suffer from retention of urine or discharge of urine by drops, feeble urination, pale complexion, coldness in lower body below waist, pale tongue, and deep and thready pulse.

Treatment:

(1) Foot massage:

The massage is applied to lung 14, spleen 34, kidney 22, liver 18, urinary bladder 24, ureter 23, urethra 51 and prostate gland 50 reflecting areas (Fig. 68).

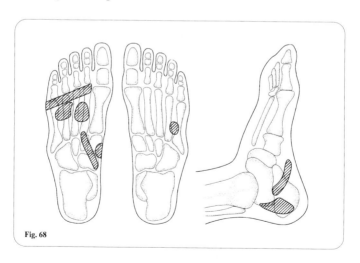

Fig. 68

(2) Foot acupuncture:

1) Meridianal acupoints: At Dazhong (KI 4), Shuiquan (KI 5), Taichong (LR 3), Yongquan (KI 1) and Zhiyin (BL 67) acupoints, a moderate reducing technique with moxibustion after acupuncture is applied and the needles are retained for 30 minutes for patients with retention of urine, except those with kidney qi deficiency to whom a reinforcing technique is applied.

2) Foot acupoints: At Uterus (FA-P 16), Urinary bladder (FA-P 15), Kidney (FA-P 14) and Spleen (FA-P 10) acupoints, a moderate twisting stimulation is applied and the needles are retained for 30 minutes. The Lung (FA-P 6) acupoint is added for patients with accumulation of heat pathogens in lung, and the Liver (FA-P 9) acupoint is added for patients with liver qi stagnation.

(3) External application of drugs:

1) Dysuria: The powder of alum 31 gm is mixed with vinegar to prepare a paste for application over the central area of both soles, once a day.

2) Retention of urine with distension of lower abdomen: One bulb of Shuixian (Chinese sacred lily) and 30 grains of Bimazi (castor bean) with skin peeled are pounded to prepare a paste for application over the central area of both soles and changed 2-3 times each night.

3) Retention of urine: Five bulbs of garlic and 50 grains of Damazi (hemp seed) are pounded to prepare a paste for application over the central area of both soles at night, removed in the next morning, for several nights until the urine retention is relieved.

(4) Foot bath:

For retention of urine due to damp-heat pathogen in urinary bladder, yellow wine 1000 ml is put in a basin to soak both feet for 40 to 60 minutes.

37. Incontinence of urine:

This is the involuntary discharge of urine.

Treatment:

(1) Foot massage:

The massage is applied to kidney 22, urinary bladder 24, ureter 23, prostate gland 50, urethra 51 and pituitary gland 4 reflecting areas (Fig. 69).

(2) Foot acupuncture:

1) Meridianal acupoints: At Yongquan (KI 1), Zulinqi (GB 41), Taixi (KI 3), Taichong (LR 3) and Zhongfeng (LR 4)

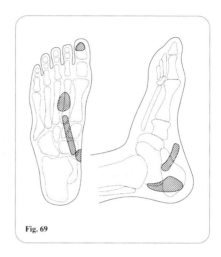

Fig. 69

acupoints, a moderate balanced reinforce-reducing technique is applied and the needles are retained for 30 minutes.

2) Foot acupoints: At Urinary bladder (FA-P 15) and Kidney (FA-P 14) acupoints, a moderate twisting stimulation is applied and the needles are retained for 30 minutes.

38. Low fever:

This is a symptom with body temperature between 37.4 and 38 degrees centigrade. The patient may have fever at irregular times subjective feverishness, and a hot feeling in palms and soles.

Differential diagnosis: Patients with liver qi stagnation may suffer from annoyance, distension in chest and subcostal region, sighing, irregular menstruation with abdominal pain, and distension of breasts. Patients with blood stasis may suffer from afternoon or night fever, dryness in mouth without desire to drink water, fixed tender spots or masses on the trunk or limbs, sallow complexion, purple tongue, and uneven pulse. Patients with deficiency of qi may suffer from instant fever, dizziness, weakness of body, shortness of breath, no desire to speak, passage of loose stool, pale tongue with thin and white coating, and thready and weak pulse. Patients with blood deficiency may suffer from dizziness, insomnia, heart palpitations, chest distress, sallow complexion, pale lips and nails, pale tongue and thready pulse. And patients with Yin deficiency may suffer from afternoon or night fever, hot feeling in palms and soles, annoyance, insomnia, dreaminess, flushed cheeks, spontaneous sweating during sleep, dryness in mouth, dry and red tongue or with fissures, with scanty or no tongue coating, and thready and rapid pulse. Low fever in chronic patients, postpartum women or postoperative patients may be treated by the following methods.

Treatment:

(1) Foot massage:

The massage is applied to head 1, brain stem and cerebellum 3, pituitary gland 4, frontal sinus 2, liver 18, kidney 22, spleen 34, lymph nodes (upper body, 39), lymph nodes (abdomen, 40) and lymph nodes (chest, 41) reflecting areas (Fig. 70).

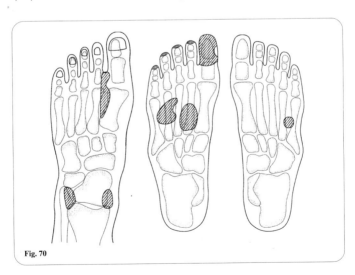

Fig. 70

127

(2) Foot acupuncture:

Meridianal acupoints: At Neiting (ST 44), Chongyang (ST 42), Lidui (ST 45), Zuqiaoyin (GB 44), Zutonggu (BL 66) and Zhiyin (BL 67) acupoints, a reducing technique is applied to patients with liver qi stagnation or blood stasis, and a balanced reinforce- reducing technique is applied to patients with qi, blood or Yin deficiency and the needles are retained for 30 minutes. Moxibustion after acupuncture is applied to patients with qi or blood deficiency.

39. Trigeminal neuralgia:

Patients with trigeminal neuralgia may suffer from a sudden onset of severe paroxysmal, spastic, cutting or pricking pain over the innervating areas of the trigeminal nerve, including forehead, upper and lower lips, and nasal or orbital region. At the beginning, the duration of the attack is short and the interval between attacks is long, and then the duration is gradually prolonged and the frequency and severity of attacks are gradually increased. The attacks are often induced by emotional distress, cold or hot stimulation, chewing food, washing the face, brushing the teeth or speaking.

Differential diagnosis: Patients whose symptoms are caused by wind and cold pathogens may suffer from paroxysmal attacks of pain aggravated by cold stimulation and alleviated by heat, pale complexion, edema of face, pale tongue with white coating, and tense pulse. Patients with fire pathogens in liver and stomach may suffer from burning pain on face, flushed face, red eyes with much eye residue, restlessness, anger, thirst, constipation, yellow and dry tongue coating, and wiry and rapid pulse. And patients with qi deficiency and blood stagnation may suffer from repeated attacks of facial pain over some years, pathological leanness of body, shallow breath, no desire to speak, aggravation of attacks after fatigue, red tongue with scanty coating, and thready and weak pulse.

Treatment:

(1) Foot massage:

The massage is applied to head 1, frontal sinus 2, liver 18, stomach 15, kidney 22, eye 8, ear 9, palate 47 and lower jaw 46 reflecting areas (Fig. 71).

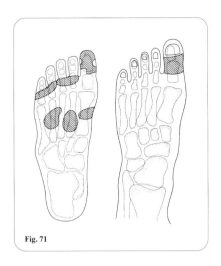

Fig. 71

(2) Foot acupuncture:
1)Meridianal acupoints: At Lidui (ST 45), Jiexi (ST 41), Chongyang (ST 42), Xiaxi (GB 43), Taixi (KI 3) and Xingjian (LR 2) acupoints, a moderate reducing technique is applied and the needles are retained for 20 minutes.

2) Foot acupoints: A moderate twisting stimulation is applied at Face (FA-P 4) acupoint for all patients with trigeminal neuralgia, and Liver (FA-P 9) and Stomach (FA-P 8) acupoints are added for patients with fire pathogens in liver and stomach. Moxibustion after acupuncture is applied to patients attacked by wind and cold pathogens.

40. Proctoptosis:

Prolapse of the anus or rectum is usually caused by constipation or chronic diarrhea, hemorrhoids, weakness in aged people, women after childbirth, and fatigue or crying in children.

Differential diagnosis: Patients of the excessive type may suffer from constipation, redness, swelling, itching or pricking pain of anus, abdominal distension, red tongue with yellow coating, and rapid pulse. Patients of the deficient type may suffer from weakness, shallow breath, no desire to speak, mental fatigue, sallow complexion, poor appetite, vertigo, pale tongue with thin coating, and soft and thready pulse.

Treatment:

(I)Footmassage:

The massage is applied to kidney 22, ascending, transverse and descending colon 28, 29 and 30,rectum 31, anus 32, spleen 34 and stomach 15 reflecting areas (Fig.72).

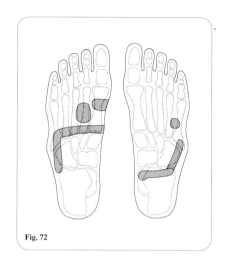

Fig. 72

(2) Foot acupuncture:

Meridianal acupoints: At Shugu (BL 65), Taichong (LR 3), Jiexi (ST 41) and Taibai (SP 3) acupoints, a reducing technique is applied to patients of the excessive type and a reinforcing technique with moxibustion after acupuncture is applied to patients of the deficient type.

(3) External application of drug:

Bimazi (castor bean) 15 gm is pounded to prepare a paste for ap plication over the central area of both soles, affixed with adhesive plaster.

41. Stiff neck:

Pain and limited neck movement may be relieved through self-healing within 4-5 days in mild cases. But it may radiate to the shoulder, back and occipital region and last for several weeks in severe cases. Differential diagnosis: Patients attacked by wind and cold pathogens may suffer from chills and pain in neck, relievable by heat, pale tongue with white coating, and floating pulse. Patients whose condition is caused by external trauma may suffer from local pain, pale tongue, and wiry pulse.

130

Treatment:

(1) Foot massage:

The massage is applied to neck 7, cervical spine 53, trapezius muscle 11 and kidney 22 reflecting areas (Fig. 73).

(2) Foot acupuncture:

1) Meridianal acupoints: At Jinggu (BL 64), Shugu (BL 65), Kunlun (BL 60), Qiuxu (GB 40) and Lidui (ST 45) acupoints, a strong reducing technique is applied and the needles are retained for 20 minutes. Moxibustion after acupuncture is applied to patients attacked by wind and cold pathogens.

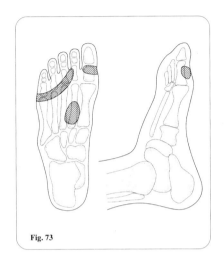

Fig. 73

2) Foot acupoint: Moderate lifting, thrusting and twisting stimulation of the reducing technique is applied at Stiff neck (FA-D 6) acupoint and the needle is retained for 20 minutes. Moxibustion after acupuncture is applied to patients whose condition is caused by wind and cold pathogens.

42. Carsickness:

Patients may suffer from dizziness, headache, nausea, vomiting, sweating, general weakness, and pale complexion.

Treatment:

(1) Foot massage:

The massage is applied to head 1, brain stem and cerebellum 3 coeliac plexus 20, spleen 34, stomach 15 and balance organ (labyrinth, 42) reflecting areas (Fig. 74).

(2) Foot acupuncture:

Meridianal acupoints: At Yongquan (KI 1), Jiexi (ST 41), Dazhong

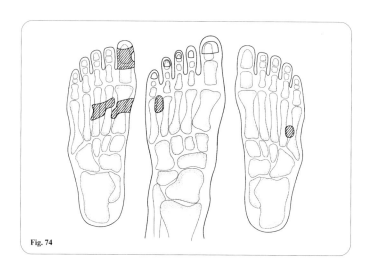

Fig. 74

(KI 4), Taibai (SP 3) and Dadu (SP 2) acupoints, a reducing technique and moxibustion after acupuncture is applied.

43. Obesity:

Differential diagnosis: Patients with deficiency of spleen and damp
stagnation may suffer from poor appetite, general weakness, shortness of breath after physical exertion, loose stool, loose and flaccid
muscles, pale and puffy tongue, and soft, moderate and weak pulse.
Patients with a strong stomach and weak spleen may suffer from
overeating, dry stool, thirst, dark urine, foul odor in mouth, high
blood pressure, red tongue with yellow and greasy coating, and
rolling and rapid or wiry and rapid pulse. And patients with disturbance of Chongmai (thoroughfare vessel) and Renmai (conceptional
vessel) may suffer from frequent urination, soreness and weakness
of waist and legs, irregular menstruation with less uterine discharge,
obese abdomen and buttocks, pale and puffy tongue, and deep and
thready or soft and thready pulse.

Treatment:

(1) Foot massage:

The massage is applied to spleen 34, Stomach 15, kidney 22, lower abdomen 37, thyroid gland 12 and pituitary gland 4 reflecting areas (Fig. 75).

(2) Foot acupuncture:

Meridianal acupoints: At Jiexi (ST 41), Neiting (ST 44), Xian'gu (ST 43), Gongsun (SP 4), Shangqiu (SP 5) and Taibai (SP 3) acupoints, a balanced reinforce-reducing technique is applied and the needles are retained for 20 minutes. Yinbai (SP 1), Dadun (LR 1), Taichong (LR 3) and Taixi (KI 3) acupoints may be added for patients with disturbance of Chongmai and Renmai, and moxibustion after acupuncture may be applied to all patients except those with strong stomach and weak spleen.

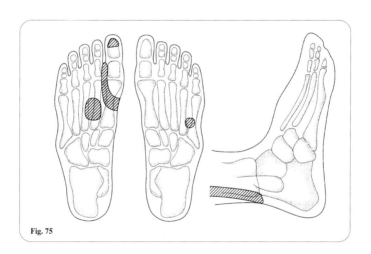

Fig. 75

II. Gynecological Diseases

1. Irregular menstruation:

A menstrual cycle moving up for more than seven days, or two menstruations in one month is called advanced menstruation. A menstrual cycle delayed for more than seven days or more is called retarded menstruation. Either condition is called irregular menstruation.

Differential diagnosis: Patients with stagnation of liver qi may suffer from amenorrhea or advanced, retarded or irregular menstrual cycle with menstrual blood and clots normal, profuse or scanty in amount, purplish red in color, sticky in nature and difficult to discharge. Patients with bleeding due to heat in blood may suffer from flushed face, red lips, advanced menstrual cycle with menstrual blood profuse or normal in amount, fresh red in color and sticky in nature. Patients with stagnation of cold pathogens in uterus may suffer from cold and pain in lower abdomen relievable by heat, cyanotic face and lips, cold limbs and retarded menstrual cycle with menstrual blood and clots normal or scanty in amount, and dark red in color. Patients with internal obstruction of stagnated blood may suffer from distension and pain in lower abdomen, relief after discharge of blood clots, and irregular menstrual cycle with profuse or scanty dark red menstrual blood and clots discharged in small amount or by drops. Patients with spleen qi deficiency may suffer from sallow complexion, mental fatigue, and amenorrhea or advanced, retarded or irregular menstrual cycle discharging pink and thin vaginal blood in large or small amount. And patients with kidney Yin deficiency may suffer from flushed cheeks, hotness in palms and soles, annoyance, insomnia and amenorrhea or advanced, retarded or irregular menstrual cycle discharging profuse or scanty and fresh red and sticky vaginal blood.

Treatment:

(1) Foot massage:

The massage is applied to pituitary gland 4, kidney 22, reproductive gland 36, uterus 50, lower abdomen 37, adrenal gland 21, thyroid gland 12 and coeliac plexus 20 reflecting areas. The foot is held with one hand by the physician and the massage is applied with the knuckle of the flexed index finger of the other hand by pressing the selected areas 3-4 times or by scratching the sole from heel to toes 5-6 times (Fig. 76).

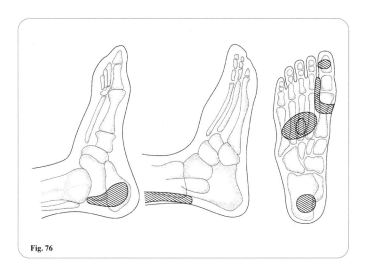

Fig. 76

(2) Foot acupuncture:

1) Meridianal acupoints: A balanced reinforce-reducing technique without moxibustion is applied at Taichong (LR 3) and Taixi (KI 3) acupoints for patients with advanced menstrual cycle. Acupuncture with moxibustion is applied at Rangu (KI 2) and Yinbai (SP 1) acupoints for patients with irregular menstruation and the needles are retained for 30 minutes.

2) Extra acupoints: A balanced reinforce-reducing technique without moxibustion is applied at 8 Yindu acupoints, Duyin (EX-F 17), Yingchi (EX-F 4) and Tongli (EX-F 11) acupoints to patients with advanced menstrual cycle. Acupuncture with moxibustion at above acupoints is applied for patients with irregular menstruation and the needles are retained for 20 minutes.

3) Foot acupoints: A balanced reinforce-reducing technique with-

out moxibustion is applied at Uterus (FA-P 16) and Dysmenorrhea 1 and 2 (FA-M 2 and 3) to patients with advanced menstrual cycle and the needles are retained for 20 minutes. A reinforcing technique of acupuncture with moxibustion is applied at above acupoints to patients with irregular menstruation and the needles are retained for 15 minutes.

(3) External application of drugs:

1) The powder of Shexiang (musk) 0.2 gm is spread over the lower abdomen 37 reflecting area on the foot and then an adequate amount of mixed powder of Ruxiang (frankincense) 15 gm, Moyao (myrrh) 15 gm, Xuejie (dragon's blood) 15 gm, Chenxiang (eagle wood) 15 gm, Dingxiang (cloves) 15 gm, Qingyan (halite) 18 gm, Wulingzhi (trogopterus dung) 18 gm and Liangtoujian (anemone) 18 gm is spread over the musk powder and covered by a piece of bark of the Chinese scholartree with small holes. Moxibustion with moxa wool is applied over the bark once a day to treat disturbance of menstruation due to liver qi stagnation.

2) A paste made of Dahuang (rhubarb) 128 gm, Xuanshen (figwort root) 64 gm, Shengdi (rehmannia root) 64 gm, Danggui (Chinese angelica root) 64 gm, Chishao (red peony root) 64 gm, Baizhi (dahurian angelica root) 64 gm and Rougui (cinnamon bark) 64 gm by trying in 1000 gm of sesame oil with 448 gm of yellow lead is applied over the lower abdomen 37 reflecting area on the foot to treat the disturbance of menstruation in patients with bleeding due to heat pathogens in blood.

3) The Shanzha (hawthorn fruit) 100 gm, Gegen (kudzuvine root) 100 gm, Baishao (white peony root) 150 gm and Gancao (licorice) 30 gm are boiled in water twice, the concentrated decoction of above herbs is mixed with an adequate amount of 95 percent alcohol extract of Ruxiang (frankincense) 100 gm and Moyao (myrrh) 100 gm; after the mixture is dried, it is mixed with the powder of Chuanshanjia (pangolin scale) 100 gm, Houpo (magnolia bark) 100 gm and Guizhi (cinnamon twig) 30 gm and an adequate amount of

Bingpian (borneol) and volatile oil of Xixin (wild ginger) and Jishiteng (chicken-dung) for use after sifting out. The powder of 0.2-0.25 gm is mixed with vinegar and applied over the reflecting area of foot 3-5 days before the start of menstruation for patients with stagnation of qi and blood. This powder mixed with ginger juice is used for patients with an accumulation of cold and damp pathogens.

2. Dysmenorrhea:

This is a disease in women including pain or severe pain in lower abdomen and waist before, during and/or after menstruation.

Differential diagnosis: Patients with cold stagnation and damp pathogens may suffer from cold and pain in lower abdomen before or during menstruation aggravated by pressing and alleviated by heat, with a small amount of dark blood and clots, thin and white tongue coating, and deep and tense pulse. Patients with liver qi stagnation may suffer from more distension and less pain in lower abdomen before or during menstruation with difficult discharge of a small amount of blood and clots, distension and pain in chest, breasts and flank, dark tongue with petechiae and thin and white coating, and deep and wiry pulse. Patients with deficiency of liver and kidney may suffer from dull pain in lower abdomen reducible by pressing during or after menstruation, with discharge of thin and pink blood, soreness and pain of back and waist, pale complexion, pale tongue, and deep and thready pulse.

Treatment:

(1) Foot massage:

The massage is applied to kidney 22, pituitary gland 4, reproductive gland 36, inguinal groove 49 and lower abdomen 37 reflecting areas. The pressing maneuver is applied on kidney area first, the pressing and kneading maneuvers are applied on pituitary gland and inguinal groove areas and the reproductive gland and lower abdomen areas are pressed and kneaded in particular (Fig. 77).

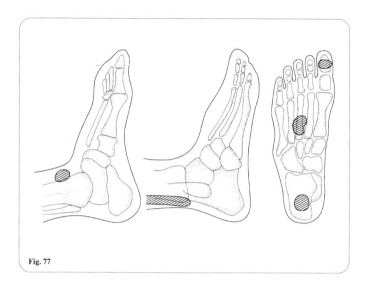

Fig. 77

(2) Foot acupuncture:

1) Meridianal acupoints: At Neiting (ST 44), Zuqiaoyin (GB 44) and Shuiquan (KI 5) acupoints, a balanced reinforce-reducing technique is applied and the needles are retained for 20 minutes. Moxibustion is applied for 10 to 20 minutes at each of above acupoints after acupuncture for patients with stagnation of cold and damp pathogens. This treatment can produce a good therapeutic result during an attack of pain.

2) Extra acupoint: At Quchi (EX-F 10) acupoint, a balanced reinforce-reducing technique is applied and the needle is retained for 20 minutes. Moxibustion for 10 to 20 minutes is applied after acupuncture for patients with stagnation of cold and damp pathogens.

3) Foot acupoints: At Uterus (FA-P 16) and Dysmenorrhea 2 (FA-M 3) acupoints, a balanced reinforce-reducing technique is applied and the needles are retained for 20 minutes. Moxibustion for 10 to 20 minutes after acupuncture is applied at each acupoint to patients with stagnation of cold and damp pathogens.

138

(3) External application of drugs:

1) For stagnation of cold and damp pathogens: Table salt 300 gm, fresh ginger (cut) 120 gm and a handful of green onions are fried and the hot paste is applied over the lower abdomen 37 reflecting area on foot.

After the sole is cleaned with a wet towel, the powder of Baizhi (dahurian angelica root) 6 gm, Wulingzhi (trogopterus dung) 6 gm and Qingyan (halite) 6 gm is spread over the correspondent reflecting areas and covered by a piece of fresh ginger for application of moxibustion, every other day.

2) For stagnation of qi and blood: Gegen (kudzuvine root) 100 gm and Baishao (white peony root) 150 gm are boiled in water twice to prepare a paste and then mixed with the extract of Ruxiang (frankincense) 100 gm and Moyao (myrrh) 100 gm in 95 percent alcohol. After drying, it is mixed with the powder of Chuanshanjia (pangolin scale) 100 gm, Houpo (magnolia bark) 100 gm and an adequate amount of volatile oil of Xixin (wild ginger) for use after thorough mixing and sifting out. The powder is mixed with vinegar to prepare a paste for application over the lower abdomen 37 foot reflecting area to treat patients with stagnation of qi and blood, and mixed with ginger juice to treat patients with stagnation of cold and damp pathogens.

3. Functional uterine bleeding:

This is a condition with a variety of menstrual disturbances in adolescents or menopausal period with profuse or dripping discharge of vaginal blood not related to the menstrual cycle. It may be caused by damage and deficiency of the spleen and stomach qi due to improper diet or fatigue and impaired preservation of blood in Chongmai (thoroughfare vessel) and Renmai (conception vessel) in patients with deficiency of spleen; by deficiency of kidney Yang and impaired preservation of blood in Chongmai and Renmai; by deficiency of kidney Yin, disturbed movement of deficient fire and impaired preservation of blood; by invasion of external heat pathogens or intake of too much spicy food damaging Chongmai and Renmai and the normal circulation of blood in patients with excessive Yang; by stagnation of liver qi and production of fire from stagnant qi disturbing the preservation of blood; or by accumulation of damp-heat pathogens in Xiajiao (lower energizer) damaging vessels of the uterus and causing uterine bleeding.

Differential diagnosis: Patients with heat pathogens in blood may suffer from discharge of dark red vaginal blood with foul odor, dryness in mouth with desire to drink water, red tongue with yellow coating, and rolling and rapid pulse. Patients with damp-heat pathogens may suffer from discharge of dark red vaginal blood with much leukorrhea and foul odor, pudendal itching, yellow and greasy tongue coating, and soft and rapid pulse. Patients with blood stasis may suffer from discharge of blood with clots, abdominal pain relieved after discharge of clots, dark red tongue, and deep and uneven pulse. Patients with accumulation of heat may suffer from distension and pain in chest and flank, annoyance, anger, frequent sighing, and wiry and rapid pulse. Patients with qi deficiency may suffer from discharge of pink vaginal blood, pale complexion, fatigue, shortness of breath, pale tongue with thin and white coating, and thready pulse. Patients with deficiency of Yang may suffer from discharge of pink vaginal blood, cold and pain in lower abdomen, cold limbs, preference for heat and aversion to cold, pale tongue with white coating, and deep and thready pulse. And patients with Yin deficiency may suffer from discharge of scanty fresh red vaginal blood, hotness in heart, palms and soles, insomnia, night sweating, soreness and weakness of waist and knees, red tongue with scanty coating, and thready and rapid pulse.

Treatment:

(1) Foot massage:

The massage is applied to pituitary gland 4, adrenal gland 21, coeliac plexus 20, kidney 22, lower abdomen 37 and reproductive gland 36 reflecting areas. The foot is held by the physician with one hand and the knuckle of the first interphalangeal joint of the index finger of the other hand is used to apply pressure 3-4 times on each of the above areas or to scratch the sole from heel to toes 5-6 times (Fig. 78).

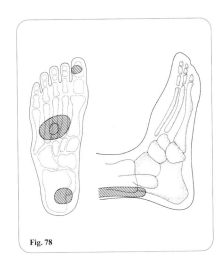

Fig. 78

(2) Foot acupuncture:

1) Meridianal acupoints: Besides Yinbai (SP 1), Shuiquan (KI 5) is added for heat pathogens in blood; Taixi (KI 3) is added for deficiency of Yin; and Dadu (SP 2) is added for deficiency of qi. A reducing technique without moxibustion is applied to patients with excessive heat pathogens, and a reinforcing technique with moxibustion for 15 to 20 minutes is applied to patients with excessive cold pathogens.

2) Extra acupoint: At Sole (EX-F 18) acupoint a reducing technique without moxibustion is applied to patients with excessive heat pathogens; and a reinforcing technique and moxibustion is applied for patients with excessive cold pathogens. The needle is retained for 15 to 20 minutes and the moxa cone is changed 3-5 times.

3) Foot acupoints: At Dysmenorrhea 1 and 2 (FA-M 2 and 3) acupoints, a reinforcing technique is applied for deficient type of disease and the reducing technique is used for excessive types of disease; the needles are retained for 20 minutes, and gentle moxibustion is applied for 15 to 20 minutes to patients with excessive cold pathogens.

(3) External application of drug:

One piece of Bimaye (castor leaf) is pounded to prepare a paste for application over lower abdomen 37 and kidney 22 reflecting areas on foot. The paste is changed once a day.

4. Leukorrhagia:

This condition involves the disturbed discharge of leukorrhea in abnormal amounts, color, odor and nature. In traditional Chinese medicine it includes white, blue, and yellow leukorrhea.

Differential diagnosis: Patients with spleen deficiency may suffer from lingering discharge of white or light yellow sticky leukorrhea without foul odor, cold limbs, pale tongue with white and greasy coating, and moderate to weak pulse. Patients with kidney Yang deficiency may suffer from continuous discharge of white, profuse, thin and cold leukorrhea, severe waist pain, coldness in lower abdomen, pale tongue with thin and white coating, and deep and slow pulse. Patients with kidney Yin deficiency may suffer from discharge of red or white sticky leukorrhea without foul odor, annoyance, hotness in heart, palms and soles, red tongue with scanty coating, and thready to rapid pulse. Patients with damp-heat pathogens may suffer from discharge of profuse, yellow or yellowish white and sticky leukorrhea with foul odor, reduced discharge of dark urine, yellow and greasy tongue coating, and soft and rapid pulse. And patients with toxic heat pathogens may suffer from discharge of profuse, sticky and foul leukorrhea with a mixed color of red, white or other colors, annoyance and hotness in body, dryness in mouth, passage of dry stool, discharge of short streams of dark urine, red tongue with yellow coating, and rapid pulse.

Treatment:

(1) Foot massage:

The massage is applied to uterus 50, vagina 51 and kidney 22 reflecting areas. The foot is held by the physician with one hand and the knuckle of the first interphalangeal joint of the other flexed index finger is used to apply massage to the sole from toes to heel 4-6 times (Fig. 79).

(2) Foot acupuncture:

1) Meridianal acupoints: A reducing technique without moxibustion is applied at Yinbai (SP 1) and Xingjian (LR 2) to patients with damp-heat pathogens and the needles are retained for 20 minutes. A balanced rein-

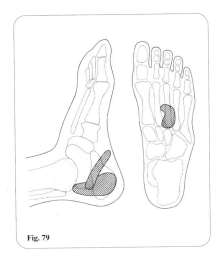

Fig. 79

force-reducing technique with moxibustion is applied at Yinbai to patients with cold and damp pathogens and the moxa cone is changed 3-5 times.

2) Extra acupoints: At Yingchi (EX-F 4) and Yinyang (EX-F 5) acupoints, a reducing technique without moxibustion is applied to patients with damp-heat pathogens and the needles are retained for 20 minutes. A balanced reinforce-reducing technique with moxibustion is applied to patients with cold and damp pathogens and the moxa cone is changed 3-5 times.

3) Foot acupoints: At Uterus (FA-P 16) and Dysmenorrhea 1 and 2 (FA-M 2 and 3) acupoints, a reducing technique without moxibustion is applied to patients with damp-heat pathogens, and a balanced reinforce-reducing technique with moxibustion is applied to patients with cold and damp pathogens. The needles are retained for 20 minutes and the moxa cone is changed 3-5 times.

(3) External application of drugs:

1) Recipe A: Liuhuang (sulphur) 18 gm, Mudingxiang (clove fruit) 15 gm, Shexiang (musk) 3 gm, Zhusha (cinnabar) 3 gm and 2 bulbs

of single bulb garlic (peeled); and Recipe B: Chuanjiao (prickly-ash peel) 50 gm, Jiucaizi (Chinese leek seed) 20 gm, Chenpi (tangerine peel) 20 gm, Rougui (cinnamon bark) 20 gm, Shechuangzi (cnidium fruit) 20 gm, single bulb garlic 300 gm, sesame oil 500 ml and Guangdan 250 gm.

The powder of herbs in Recipe A is pounded with garlic to prepare a paste. The herbs in Recipe B are fried in sesame oil until they are charred and removed, and then Guangdan is slowly added to the boiling oil until the oil is concentrated to produce a paste. The pastes are applied over the uterus 50 and vagina 51 reflecting areas on foot for the patients with cold and damp pathogens.

2) The powder of Baijiguanhua (white cockscomb, fried with vinegar), Honghua (safflower, fried with alcohol), Baizhu (bighead Atractylodes rhizome), Heyehui (ash of lotus leaf), Fuling (Indian bread) and Cheqianzi (plantain seed) in same proportion is mixed with yellow wine to prepare a paste for application over kidney 22, uterus 50 and vagina 51 reflecting areas on foot and wrapped with gauze and adhesive plaster for patients with damp-heat pathogens. The powder is changed every other day.

5. Amenorrhea:

This is a gynaecological condition found in women over 18 years of age without menarche, or in women whose regular menstruation has stopped for over three months.

Differential diagnosis: Patients with depletion of blood may suffer from gradual retardation of menstruation and gradual reduction of vaginal discharge until the menstrual flow is stopped. If accompanied by dizziness, tinnitus, soreness and weakness of waist and knees, dryness in mouth and throat, hotness in heart, palms and soles, tidal fever with sweating, red tongue, and wiry and thready pulse, it is caused by deficiency of liver and kidney. If accompanied by heart palpitations, mental fatigue and physical weakness, loss of appetite, passage of loose stool, pale tongue, and thready and weak pulse, it is caused by deficiency of spleen and stomach. And if accompanied by pale complexion, pathological leanness of body, pale tongue, and thready pulse, it is caused by blood deficiency. Patients with stagnation of qi and blood may suffer from amenorrhea, mental depression, restlessness, anger, distension of chest and flank, distension of lower abdomen with pain, dark purple tongue with petechiae, and deep and wiry pulse. Patients with co-agulation of blood by cold pathogens may suffer from cold body and limbs, cold and pain in lower abdomen, white tongue coating, and deep and slow pulse. Patients with blockage of phlegm and dampness may suffer from obesity, distress and fullness in chest and flank, mental and physical fatigue, profuse discharge of leukorrhea, greasy tongue coating, and rolling pulse.

Treatment:

(1) Foot massage:

The massage is applied to pituitary gland 4, kidney 22, reproductive gland 36, thyroid gland 12, coeliac plexus 20 and adrenal gland 21 reflecting areas. The foot is held by the phy sician with one hand and the knuckle of flexed first interphalangeal joint of the other

index finger is used to apply massage from the toes to heel or on the correspondent refl-ecting areas on foot 4-6 times (Fig. 80).

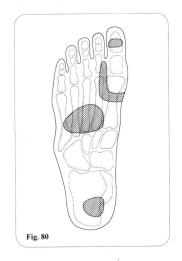

Fig. 80

(2) Foot acupuncture:

Meridianal acupoints: At Xiaxi (GB 43),

Shuiquan (KI 5), Dadun (LR 1) and Xingjian (LR 2) acupoints, a reinforcing technique with moxibustion is applied to pa-tients with depletion of blood, and a reducing technique without moxibustion is applied to patients with stagnation of blood. The needles are retained for 20 minutes and the moxa cone is changed 3-5 times.

(3) External application of drugs:

1) Dahuang (rhubarb) 128 gm, Mangxiao (sodium sulfate) 64 gm, Chaihu (thorowax root) 32 gm, Gualou (snakegourd root) 32 gm, Taoren (peach kernel) 32 gm, Danggui (Chinese angelica root) 32 gm, Shengdi (rehmannia root) 32 gm, Honghua (safflower) 32 gm, Chuanshanjia (pangolin scale) 32 gm, Erzhu (zedoary tumeric) 32 gm, Sanleng (burreed tuber) 32 gm, Chuanxiong (Szechuan lovage) 32 gm, Ruxiang (frankincense) 22 gm, Moyao (myrrh) 22 gm, Rougui (cinnamon bark) 22 gm and Chuanwu (aconite root) 10 gm are fried in sesame oil with Huangdan (yellow lead) and finally mixed with Huaruishi (ophicalcite) 32 gm and Xuejie (dragon's blood) 15 gm to prepare a paste for application over the reproductive gland 36 and other correspondent reflecting areas on foot for patients with qi and blood stagnation.

2) The powder of Hujiao (white pepper) 9 gm, Huangdan (yellow lead) 9 gm and Huoxiao (saltpetre) 9 gm is mixed to prepare three small cakes for application over the reproductive gland 36 and other correspondent reflecting areas on foot for patients with accumulation of cold and damp pathogens.

3) Fresh Wutongpi (bark of Chinese parasol tree) 150 gm is boiled in water with Awei (asafetida) 90 gm to prepare a paste for application over the coeliac plexus 20 and other related reflecting areas on foot.

6. Prolapse of uterus:

Prolapse of the uterus usually appears after childbirth in women with many children. Mild cases are called vaginocele with prolapse of vaginal wall, and severe cases are called prolapse of uterus with the uterine cervix protruding out of the vaginal orifice. In traditional Chinese medicine this is considered caused by damage to the uterus vessels due to descending spleen qi or a deficiency of the kidney in failing to keep the internal organs in their normal positions. Differential diagnosis: Patients with descending spleen qi may suffer from prolapse of uterus out of the vaginal orifice, more pronounced when fatigued, spastic sensation in lower abdomen, weakness of limbs, shallow breath, no desire to speak, sallow complexion, pale tongue with thin and white coating, and feeble and thready pulse. And patients with deficiency of kidney may suffer from prolapse of uterus, soreness and weakness of waist and legs, spastic sensation in lower abdomen, frequent urination, dizziness, tinnitus, pink tongue with thin and white coating, and deep and weak pulse.

Treatment:

(1) Foot massage: The massage is applied to uterus 50 and va gina 51 reflecting areas with the pad of thumb 3-4 times, or with the medial border of flexed index finger to scratch or press 3-4 times (Fig. 81).

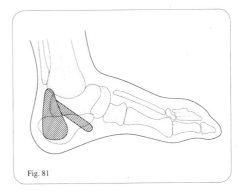

Fig. 81

(2) Foot acupuncture:

Meridianal acupoint: A reinforcing technique of acupuncture with moxibustion is applied at Shuiquan (KI 5) acupoint, the needle is retained for 15-20 minutes, and the moxa cone is changed 3-5 times.

(3) External application of drugs:

1) An adequate amount of hot Shechuangzi (cnidium root) after frying is applied over uterus 50 reflecting area on foot to treat prolapse of uterus with severe pain.

2) Hot paste of Bimazi (castor seed) 60 gm, Aiye (mugwort) 30 gm, Zaoxintu (furnace soil) 60 gm and Hubo (amber) 9 gm is applied to uterus 50 reflecting area on foot.

3) The powder of Heshouwu (cornbind) 30 gm is wrapped in white cloth and put into the cavity of a killed cock 3000 gm in weight, and after it is well cooked by steaming, the chicken meat and soup is eaten and drunk twice. The chicken bone and Heshouwu are then pounded to prepare a paste for application over the uterus 50 and vagina 51 reflecting areas on foot. This method can effectively treat the prolapse of uterus after childbirth for half a month without any complications.

7. Pudendal itching:

This is an intractable itching in the perineal region and vagina, radiated to medial side of thigh and causing restlessness and profuse discharge of leukorrhea, annoyance, bitter taste in mouth, and dizziness and vertigo. It is caused by spleen deficiency, and accumulation of excessive dampness, the stagnation of liver qi producing heat pathogens, a combination of dampness and heat and downward pouring of damp-heat pathogens; or it may be caused by poor hygiene of external genitalia, sitting on damp ground too long, or a parasite infection in perineal region.

Treatment:

(1) Foot massage:

The massage is applied to kidney 22, ureter 23, urinary bladder 24, adrenal gland 21, uterus 50, reproductive gland 36 and vagina 51 reflecting areas. The foot is held by the physician with one hand and the knuckle of the first interphalangeal joint of the other flexed index finger is used to apply mas-

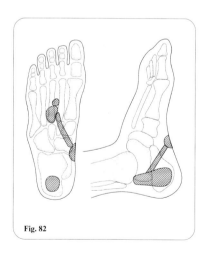

Fig. 82

sage to the correspondent reflecting areas 3-4 times (Fig. 82).

(2) Foot acupuncture:

Meridianal acupoints: At Zhaohai (KI 6) and Rangu (KI 2) acupoints, a balanced reinforce-reducing acupuncture technique without moxibustion is applied and the needles are retained for 15 to 20 minutes.

(3) External application of drugs:

1) Downward pouring of damp-heat pathogens: The powder of Bianxu (knotweed) 30 gm, Yirenmi (Job's-tears seed) 20 gm, Niuxi (achyranthes root) 20 gm, Qumai (pink) 20 gm, Huashi (talc) 15 gm, Tongcao (rice paper) 15 gm and Houpo (magnolia bark) is wrapped in the sterilized gauze to make small bags in an adequate size for application on the reflecting areas on foot and changed once every other day. For severe pain, Zhizi (cape-jasmine fruit) and Longdancao (gentian) are added; for weakness of limbs, poor appetite and yellow and greasy tongue coating, Cangzhu (atractylodes rhizome) and Huoxiang (giant-hyssop) may be added; for persistent low fever with abdominal distension, Xingren (apricot kernel), Kouren (nutmeg), Danzhuye (lophatherum), Cangzhu (atractylodes rhizome), Huangbai (amur cork-tree) and Dafupi (areca peel) are added; and for patients with trichomoniasis, Shechuangzi (cnidium) 30 gm is added.

2) Infection of parasites: The powder of Xionghuang (realgar) 1 gm, fresh tobacco leaf 2 gm and small amount of alum is put into the holes of a triangular piece of pig liver (60 gm) for application on the reflecting areas on foot.

8. Pregnancy vomiting:

This is a complication in pregnant women, including nausea, vomiting, dizziness and anorexia; vomiting may occur right after eating.

Differential diagnosis: Patients with stomach deficiency may suffer from fullness and distension of upper abdomen, nausea, vomiting of food right after eating, mental fatigue and sleepiness, pale tongue with white coating, and moderate, rolling and weak pulse. Patients with heat pathogens in liver may suffer from distension and pain in chest and flank, vomiting of bitter or sour fluid, belching, sighing, distension of head and dizziness, mental depression, thin and yellow tongue coating, and wiry and rolling pulse. And patients with accumulation of phlegm may suffer from vomiting of sputum and saliva, chest distress, poor appetite, heart palpitations, shortness of breath, tastelessness in mouth, white and greasy tongue coating, and rolling pulse.

Treatment:

(1) Foot massage:

The massage is applied to pituitary gland 4 kidney 22, ureter 23, urinary bladder 24, thyroid gland 12, adrenal gland 21 and uterus 50 reflecting areas. The foot is held by the physician with one hand and the knuckle of the first interphalangeal joint of the other flexed index finger is used to apply massage to reflecting areas 3-4 times (Fig. 83).

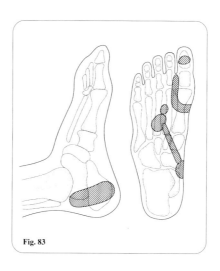

Fig. 83

(2) Foot acupuncture:

1) Meridianal acupoints: At Neiting (ST 44), Qiuxu (GB 44), Taichong (LR 3) and Gongsun (SP 4) acupoints, a reinforcing technique with moxibustion is applied for patients with stomach deficiency and a reducing technique is applied to patients with heat pathogens in liver or accumulation of phlegm. The needles are retained for 15 to 20 minutes, and moxibustion is applied for 15 minutes.

150

2) Extra acupoints: At Duyin (EX-F 17), Neihuai Qianxia (EX-F 1) and Nuxi (EX-F 6) acupoints, a reinforcing technique of acupuncture with moxibustion is applied to patients of the deficient cold type, and a reducing technique is applied to patients of the excessive heat type or with blockage of phlegm and dampness. The needles are retained for 15 to 20 minutes and moxibustion is applied for 15 minutes.

3) Foot acupoint: A reinforcing acupuncture technique with moxibustion is applied at Stomach (FA-P 8) acupoint for patients of the deficient cold type, and a reducing technique without moxibustion is applied at this acupoint for patients of the excessive heat type or with blockage of phlegm and dampness. The needles are retained for 15 to 20 minutes, and moxibustion is applied for 15 minutes.

9. Chronic pelvic inflammation:
This is a general inflammation of the female reproductive organs (uterus, oviduct and ovary) and their surrounding connective tissue. Acute patients may suffer from fever, and pain and tenderness in lower abdomen; and chronic patients may suffer from soreness of waist, disturbance of menstruation and infertility. It is included as one of the abdominal pain from abdominal tumor diseases in traditional Chinese medicine.

Differential diagnosis: Patients with deficiency of liver and kidney Yin may suffer from dull pain in lower abdomen, profuse, thin and yellow leukorrhea, soreness and weakness of waist and knees, dizziness, red tongue with scanty coating, and deep, thready and rapid pulse. And patients with deficiency of qi and blood may suffer from dull pain in lower abdomen, sallow complexion, general weakness, poor appetite, retarded menstruation with small amounts of pale vaginal discharge, pale tongue with scanty coating, and feeble pulse.

Treatment:
(1) Foot massage:

The massage is applied to reproductive gland 36, uterus 50, kidney 22, lower abdomen 37, pituitary gland 4, ureter 23, urinary bladder 24, adrenal gland 21, thyroid gland 12 and parathyroid gland 13 reflecting areas. The foot is held in one hand by the physician and the knuckle of the first interphalangeal joint of the other flexed index finger is used to apply massage on the related reflecting areas 3-4 times (Fig. 84).

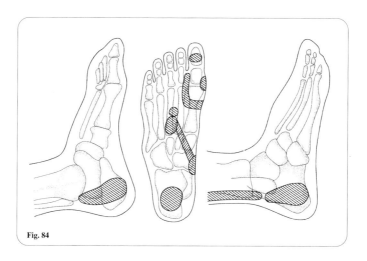

Fig. 84

(2) Foot acupuncture:
1) Meridianal acupoints: At bilateral Zulinqi (GB 41), Zhongfeng (LR 4), Taixi (KI 3) and Rangu (KI 2) acupoints, a reinforcing technique of acupuncture with moxibustion is applied, the needles are retained for 20 minutes, and moxibustion is applied for 15 minutes.
2) Foot acupoints: A reinforcing acupuncture technique with moxibustion is applied at Dysmenorrhea 2 (FA-M 3) acupoint, the needle is retained for 15 to 20 minutes, and moxibustion is applied for 15 minutes.
(3) External application of drugs: The powder of an adequate amount of Chuanjiao (prickly-ash peel), Dahuixiang (star anise), Ruxiang

(frankincense), Moyao (myrrh) and Jiangxiang (rose wood) is mixed with wheat flour and liquor to prepare a paste for application on reproductive gland 36 reflecting area after it is spread on a piece of gauze and a hot water bag is put over the drug applied on the reproductive gland reflecting area for foot massage, twice a day. This treatment is used to treat patients with inflammation and masses in pelvic cavity not curable by the oral administration of drugs.

10. Infertility in women:

Infertility in women is a reproductive condition affecting women who have failed to become pregnant after living with their husbands for more than two years, and whose husbands have normal reproductive ability, without contraceptive intervention. It may be caused by kidney deficiency, stagnation of liver, accumulation of dampness and phlegm, or blood stasis.

Differential diagnosis: Patients with kidney deficiency may suffer from retarded menstruation with discharge of reduced amounts of pink vaginal blood, reduction of sexual desire, and soreness and weakness of waist and knees. Patients with Yang deficiency may suffer from cold body and limbs, cold and pain in lower abdomen, pale tongue with white coating, and deep, slow and weak pulse. Patients with Yin deficiency may suffer from hotness in heart, palms and soles, dizziness, heart palpitations, yellow tongue coating, and wiry pulse. Patients with deficiency of qi and blood may suffer from discharge of pink vaginal blood in varied amounts, sallow complexion, fatigue, pale tongue with white coating, and deep and thready pulse. Patients with liver qi stagnation may suffer from purple menstrual discharge varied in amount and duration and mixed with clots, distension and pain in chest and flank, red tongue with white coating, and wiry pulse. Patients with accumulation of dampness and phlegm may suffer from irregular menstruation with discharge of reduced amounts of pink vaginal blood and profuse, white and thin leukorrhea, distension of chest and abdomen, poor appetite, passage of loose stool, puffy tongue with white and greasy coating, and rolling pulse. Patients with cold pathogens in uterus and blood stasis may suffer from irregular menstruation with discharge of dark red vaginal blood and clots, coldness and pain in lower abdomen during menstrual cycle, dark tongue with white coating and ecchymoses, and deep pulse. And patients with accumulation of damp-heat pathogens may suffer from pain in lower abdomen more severe before start of menstrual cycle, low fever, profuse yellow leukorrhea, dripping discharge of menstrual blood, yellow and greasy tongue coating, and rolling and rapid pulse.

Treatment:

(1) Foot massage:

The massage is applied to pituitary gland 4, kidney 22, reproductive gland 36, uterus 50, vagina 51, thyroid gland 12, parathyroid gland 13, adrenal gland 21, ureter 23 and urinary bladder 24 reflecting areas. The foot is held in one hand by the physician, the big toe is pinched by the flexed index and middle fin-

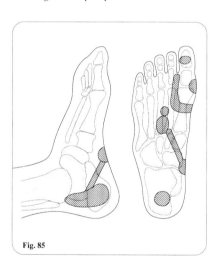

Fig. 85

gers of the other hand, the medial side of the 2nd phalangeal segment of index finger is put on the reflecting area, and the thumb is used to apply massage 3- 4 times (Fig. 85).

(2) Foot acupuncture:

Meridianal acupoints: At Yongquan (KI 1) and Rangu (KI 2) acupoints, a reinforcing technique is applied for deficient patients and a reducing technique is applied for excessive patients, and the needles

154

are retained for 15 to 20 minutes. Moxibustion for 10 to 15 minutes, after acupuncture can be applied to patients with Yang deficiency.

11. Menopausal syndrome:

This is a gynecological condition in women over 45 years old with symptoms of dysfunction of endocrinal and vegetative nervous systems due to reduction or total loss of ovarian function.

Differential diagnosis: Patients with kidney Yin deficiency may suffer from retardation of menstruation or amenorrhea, dryness in vagina, dizziness, tinnitus, insomnia, dreaminess, itching of skin, hotness in body, sweating, hotness in heart, palms and soles, unreasonable laughing and crying, anger, poor memmory, red tongue with scanty coating, and thready and rapid pulse. And patients with kidney Yang deficiency may suffer from profuse menstrual bleeding or amenorrhea, dark complexion, mental fatigue, soreness and weakness of waist and knees, cold body and limbs, edema of limbs, passage of loose stool, frequent urination or incontinence of urine, pale tongue with white coating, and deep, thready and weak pulse.

Treatment:

(1) Foot massage:

The massage is applied to head 1, neck 7, adrenal gland 21, pituitary gland 4, uterus 50, reproductive gland 36, thyroid gland 12, pancreas 17 and coeliac plexus 20 reflecting areas. The foot is held in one hand by the phy sician and the knuckle of the first interphalangeal joint of the

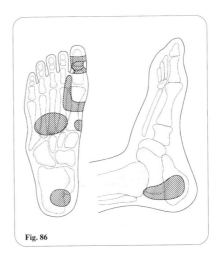

Fig. 86

other index finger is used to apply massage 3-4 times (Fig. 86).

(2) **Foot acupuncture**:

Meridianal acupoints: At Taichong (LR 3), Taixi (KI 3) and Zhaohai (KI 6) acupoints, a balanced reinforce-reducing technique is applied and the needles are retained for 15 to 20 minutes. Gentle moxibustion after acupuncture is applied for 10 to 15 minutes to deficient type patients.

12. Abnormal position of fetus:

The occital presentation is the normal position of the fetus in childbirth. Other presentations including face, breech, horizontal and arm positions are all abnormal fetal positions.

Treatment:

(1) **Foot massage**:

The massage is applied to kidney 22, reproductive gland 36, uterus 50, adrenal gland 21 and pituitary gland 4 reflecting areas. The foot is held with one hand by the physician and the knuckle of the first interphalangeal joint of the other index finger is used to apply deep pressure on the reflecting areas 3-4 times (Fig. 87).

(2) **Foot acupuncture**:

Meridianal acupoints: A balanced reinforce-reducing acupuncture technique is applied at bilateral Zhiyin (BL 67) for 15 to 20 minutes, once or twice a day, or moxibustion at both acupoints is applied for 15 to 20 minutes, once or twice a day until the abnormal fetal position is corrected.

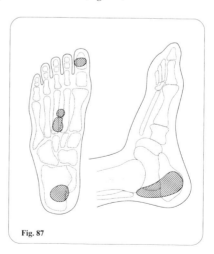

Fig. 87

(3) External application of drugs:

An adequate amount of fresh ginger and green onion is pounded to prepare a paste for application to uterus 50, reproductive gland 36 and kidney 22 reflecting areas on foot and covered by oily paper and adhesive plaster. The paste is changed every 2-3 days, 7 times, as a therapeutic course.

13. Postpartum fainting:

This is an acute disease occurring suddenly after childbirth. Its symptoms include dizziness, vertigo, difficulty in sitting up, chest distress, nausea, vomiting, accumulation of sputum in throat, shortness of breath, restlessness, and even loss of consciousness.

Differential diagnosis: Patients with blood deficiency may suffer from sudden onset of vertigo, pale complexion, heart palpitations, gradual loss of consciousness with eyes closed and mouth opened, extremely cold limbs, profuse cold sweating, pale tongue without coating, and feeble, floating or large and weak pulse. And patients with blood stasis may suffer from scanty or no lochia after childbirth, paroxysmal pain in lower abdomen, severe distension in epigastric region, shortness of breath and dyspnea, coma and loss of consciousness with hands clenched and jaw locked, cyanotic face, lips and tongue, and uneven pulse.

Treatment:

(1) Foot massage:

The massage is applied to kidney 22, heart 33, spleen 34, ureter 23 and adrenal gland 21 reflecting areas. The foot is held in one hand by the physician and the pressure is applied by the knuckle of the first interphalangeal joint of the other index finger on the

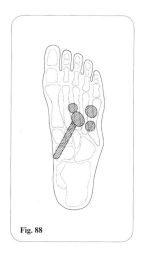

Fig. 88

157

reflecting areas 3-4 times (Fig. 88).

(2) Foot acupuncture:

1) Meridianal acupoints: At Yongquan (KI 1), Rangu (KI 2), Zhaohai (KT 6) and Xingjian (LR 2) acupoints, a reinforcing acupuncture technique or moxibustion is applied to patients with blood deficiency, and a reducing technique is applied to patients with blood stasis. The needles are retained for 15 to 20 minutes, and moxibustion is applied for 15 minutes.

2) Extra acupoints: At Xiaozhijian (tip of littie toe) and Dazhi Jumao (EX-F 14) acupoints, a reinforcing technique of acupuncture or moxibustion in applied to patients with blood deficiency, and a reducing technique is applied to patients with blood stasis. The needles are retained for 15 to 20 minutes, and moxibustion is applied for 15 minutes.

3) Foot acupuncture: A balanced reinforce-reducing technique of acupuncture is applied at Vertigo (FA-M 1) and Kidney (FA-P 14) acupoints and the needles are retained for 20 minutes. Moxibustion is applied for 10 to 15 minutes to deficient type patients.

(3) External application of drugs:

1) Deficiency of qi and blood: The powder of Chuanxiong (Szechuan lovage), Danggui (Chinese Angelica root), Huangqi (milkvetch root), Dangshen (asicebell root), Baizhu (bighead Atractylodes rhizome), Shudihuang (prepared Rehmanniaroot), Fushen (Poria cum Radice Pino), Zaoren (jujube seed) and Baiziren (arborvitae) 32 gm each and Banxia (pinellia tuber), Chenpi (tangerine peel), Maidong (lily-turf) and Gancao (licorice root) 15 gm each is applied to heart 33, kidney 22, spleen 34, adrenal gland 21 and ureter 23 reflecting areas.

2) Blood stasis: Danggui (Chinese Angelica root), Chuanxiong (Szechuan lovage), Taoren (peach kernel), Jiangtan (charred ginger), Gancao (licorice), Honghua (safflower), Yanhusuo (corydalis tuber), Rougui (cinnamon bark), Wulingzhi (trogopterus dung) and Xiangfu (nut-grass) 15 gm each are fried in sesame oil with Huangdan (yellow

158

lead) to prepare a paste for application to spleen 34 and kidney 22 reflecting areas.

14. Hypogalactia:

This is a condition in which excretion of milk in nursing mothers is insufficient to meet the demands of their babies.

Differential diagnosis: Mothers with deficiency of qi and blood may suffer from reduction or absence of milk excretion, no distending sensation in breasts, sallow complexion, dizziness, poor appetite, mental and physical fatigue, pale and puffy tongue with thin coating, and feeble and weak pulse. Mothers with liver qi stagnation may suffer from pain, distension and hotness in breasts, mental depression, chest distress, belching, thin and yellow tongue coating, and wiry pulse.

Treatment:

(1) Foot massage:

The massage is applied to lymph nodes (upper body, 39), pituitary gland 4, parathyroid gland 13, kidney 22, adrenal gland 21, chest 43, reproductive gland 36 and lymph nodes (chest, 41) reflecting areas (Fig. 89).

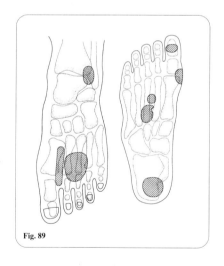
Fig. 89

(2) Foot acupuncture:
Meridianal acupoints: At Zulinqi (GB 41), Taichong (LR 3) and Diwuhui (GB 42) acupoints, a reinforcing acupuncture technique with moxibustion is applied to deficient type patients, and a reducing technique without moxibustion is applied to excessive type

patients. The needles are retained for 15 to 20 minutes, and moxibustion is applied for 10 to 15 minutes,

III. Pediatric Diseases

1. Whooping cough:

This is an acute infectious disease of the respiratory system in children. In the first 2 weeks of the disease, children may suffer from cough with thin and foamy sputum, sneezing, running nose, thin and white tongue coating, floating and strong pulse and pink finger venules; in the spastic cough period of 4-6 weeks, children may suffer from repeated attacks of paroxysmal cough with wheezing in throat and sticky sputum, worse at night; and in the recovery stage of 2-3 weeks, the frequency and duration of paroxysmal cough is reduced, wheezing gradually disappears, vomiting is also reduced, the cough becomes weak and the sputum thin and scanty, the lips are pale, the tongue is pale with scanty coating, and the finger venules are clear and pale.

Treatment:

(1) Foot massage:

The massage is applied to pituitary gland 4, lung 14, adrenal gland 21, kidney 22 and lymph nodes (upper body, 39) reflecting areas. The foot is held in one hand by the physician and the flexed first interphalangeal joint of the other index finger is

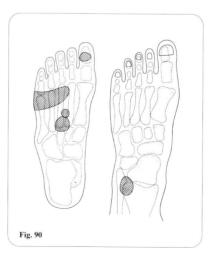

Fig. 90

160

used to apply pressure from medial side to lateral side of lung reflecting area 4-5 times, and to apply massage on other reflecting areas 3-4 times (Fig. 90).

(2) Foot acupuncture:

1) Meridianal acupoints: At Qiaoyin (GB 44) and Dazhong (KI 4) acupoints, a lifting, thrusting and twisting stimulation of reducing technique without moxibustion is applied and the needles are retained for 15 to 20 minutes.

2) Foot acupoint: A reducing acupuncture technique without moxibustion is applied at Lung (FA-P 6) acupoint and the needle is retained for 15 to 20 minutes.

(3) External application of drugs:

1) The powder of Mahuang (ephedra) 1.5 gm, wheat flour 9 gm and sweat wine 9 gm are mixed together to prepare small cakes for application on the related reflecting areas, 2-3 times a day.

2) Baibu (stemona root), Mahuang (ephedra), Baiji (bletilla tuber), Huanglian (golden thread root) and Gancao (licorice) 60 gm each and Lugen (reed) 150 gm are fried in sesame oil with Huangdan (yellow lead) to prepare a paste after the charred herbs are removed. The paste is applied once on 2-3 reflecting areas to treat the patient at an early stage of the disease or in the spastic cough period without complications.

2. Indigestive malnutrition:

This is a condition of chronic malnutrition in children under three years of age caused by the disturbance of digestion and absorption of food over a long period of time or by an insufficient intake of protein and calories.

Treatment:

(1) Foot massage:

The massage is applied to stomach 15, duodenum 16, liver 18, gallbladder 19, small intestine 25, spleen 34 and coeliac plexus 20 reflecting areas. The foot is held in one hand by the physician and the knuckle of the first interphalangeal joint of the other index finger is used to apply massage on the projecting areas 3-4 times (Fig. 91).

(2) Foot acupuncture:

1) Meridianal acupoints: At Neiting (ST 44), Gongsun (SP 4) and Shangqiu (SP 5) acupoints, a reinforcing acupuncture technique is applied and the needles are retained for 15 to 20 minutes; or moxibustion is applied for 15 minutes.

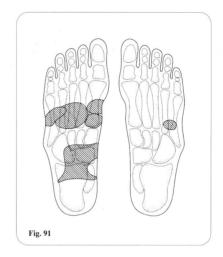

Fig. 91

2) Extra acupoint: A reinforcing acupuncture technique is applied at Ranhou (EX-F 12) acupoint and the needle is retained for 15 to 20 minutes; or moxibustion is applied for 15 minutes.

3) Foot acupoints: A reinforcing technique is applied at Stomach (FA-P 8) and Spleen (FA-P 10) acupoints and the needles are retained for 20 minutes; or moxibustion is applied for 15 minutes.

(3) External application of drugs:

1) The powder of Zhiren (cape-jasmine fruit) 30 grains, Taoren (peach kernel) 7 grains, Pixiao (sodium sulfate) 7 gm, green onion 7 pieces and 1 spoonful of fine wheat flour is mixed with the white of one egg and an adequate amount of bee honey to prepare a paste for application to spleen 34 and stomach 15 reflecting areas and covered with a piece of gauze to clear heat, promote blood circulation and resolve food stagnation. Uncooked, cold and fishy food, and desserts are prohibited for children with this disease.

2) The powder of Zhiren (cape-jasmine fruit) 30 grains, Xingren (apricot kernel) 7 gm, Hujiao (white pepper) 6 gm, green onion 7

pieces, 1 spoonful of wheat flour, and Dingxiang (cloves) 30 grains is mixed with the white of 1 egg and liquor to prepare a paste for application to the central area of both soles and covered with a piece of gauze.

3) The powder (15-20 gm) of Taoren (peach kernel), Xingren (apricot kernel) and Zhiren (cape-jasmine fruit) in same amount, and a small amount of Bingpian (borneol) and Zhangnao (camphor) is mixed with 1 egg white to prepare a paste of proper thickness for application to both Yongquan (KI 1) acupoints and wrapped with a bandage for 24 hours.

4) The powder of Xuanmingfen (exsiccated sodium sulfate) 3 gm and Hujiao (black pepper) 0.5 gm is directly applied to spleen 34 and stomach 15 reflecting areas on foot and wrapped with gauze and adhesive plaster. The powder is changed once a day.

3. Epidemic parotitis (mumps):

This is an acute epidemic disease usually occurring in winter or spring which is caused by parotitis virus and common in children between 5 and 10 years of age. It has a latent period of 2-3 weeks and clinical symptoms of fever, pain and swelling in the parotidean region.

Treatment;

(1) Foot massage:
The massage is applied to pituitary gland 4, adrenal gland 21, lymph nodes (upper body, 39), larynx 48 and tonsil 45 reflecting areas. The

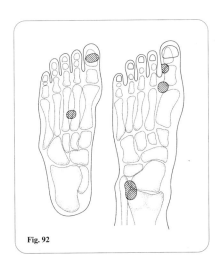

Fig. 92

foot is held in one hand by the physician and the knuckle of first interphalangeal joint of the other index finger or both thumbs are used to apply massage to the reflecting areas 3-5 times (Fig. 92).

(2) Foot acupuncture:

1) Meridianal acupoints: At Dadu (SP 2), Xian'gu (ST 43), Neiting (ST 44) and Rangu (KI 2) acupoints, a reducing technique of acupuncture without moxibustion is applied and the needles are retained for 20 minutes.

2) Foot acupoints: At Tonsil 1 and 2 (FA-D 2 and 3) and Vertigo (FA-M 1) acupoints, a reducing acupuncture technique is applied and the needles are retained for 20 to 30 minutes.

(3) External application of drugs:

1) A fine powder of 6-15 gm composed of Wuzhuyu (evodia fruit) 9 gm, Huzhang (giant knotwood rhizome) 5 gm, Zihua Diding (violet) 6 gm and Dannanxing (Jack-in-the-pulpit with ox gall) 3 gm is mixed with vinegar to prepare a paste for application to the tonsil reflecting areas, wrapped with gauze and adhesive plaster.

2) The powder of Huajiao (black pepper) 15 gm is spread on the bottom of a pot and the powder of Zhangnao (camphor) 45 gm, Bingpian (borneol) 6 gm and Mangxiao (sodium sulfate) 30 gm is spread over the Huajiao powder and covered with a clay bowel. The edge of the bowel is sealed with alum or clay mixed with table salt and the pot is baked over a low fire for 30 to 40 minutes. The white crystals obtained after the contents of the pot cools may be spread over a piece of gauze for application to the tonsil reflecting areas.

4. Bed-wetting:

This is the spontaneous discharge of urine during sleep, day or night, in children over three years of age.

Treatment:

(1) Foot massage:

The massage is applied to kidney 22, ureter 23, urinary bladder 24, urethra 51 and pituitary gland 4 reflecting areas. The area is fixed by the thumb and the medial border of the flexed index finger or the pad of thumb is used to press and scratch above the areas 3-4 times (Fig. 93).

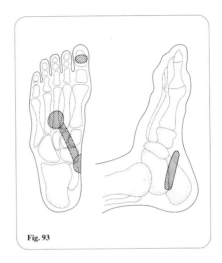

Fig. 93

(2) Foot acupuncture:

1) Meridianal acupoints: At Taichong (LR 3), Xingjian (LR 2), Shuiquan (KI 5) and Taixi (KI 3) acupoints, a reinforcing acupuncture technique or moxibustion is applied. The needles are retained for 30 minutes and moxibustion is applied for 15 minutes.

2) Foot acupoints: A reinforcing acupuncture technique or gentle moxibustion is applied at Bed-wetting (FA-P 21) acupoint. The needle is retained for 30 minutes and moxibustion is applied for 15 minutes.

(3) External application of drugs:

1) Fresh ginger 30 gm is pounded and fried hot for application to kidney 22 reflecting area before sleep.

2) An appropriate amount of Wubeizi (gallnut) powder is mixed with boiled water to prepare a paste for application to kidney 22 reflecting area.

3) Liuhuang (sulfur) powder 20 gm and green onion 120 gm are pounded together and baked to prepare a hot paste for application to kidney 22 and urinary bladder 24 reflecting areas overnight, and a hot water bag is placed over the sole. This treatment is applied 10 times.

5. Diarrhea:

In children under two years of age diarrhea is a common symptom in summer and autumn, and is usually caused by indigestion, acute gastroenteritis or enteritis.

Differential diagnosis: Babies with indigestion may suffer from abdominal distension and pain, diarrhea after onset of abdominal pain, relief of abdominal pain after diarrhea with foul stool, vomiting and indigested food, dirty and greasy tongue coating, and rolling and forceful pulse. Babies with damp-heat pathogens may suffer from diarrhea with yellow, thin and foul stool, abdominal pain, hotness in body, thirst, hotness in anus, discharge of short streams of dark urine, yellow and greasy tongue coating, and rolling and rapid pulse. And babies with Yang deficiency may suffer from repeated diarrhea, often after meals, with undigested food in thin stool, or chronic diarrhea over a long time, poor appetite, mental and physical fatigue, sallow complexion, very cold limbs, incomplete closure of eyes during sleep, pale tongue with white coating, and thready and moderate pulse.

Treatment:

(1) Foot massage:

The massage is applied to coeliac plexus 20, small intestine 25, stomach 15, colon 28-30, duodenum 16, liver 18, gallbladder 19 and spleen 34 reflecting areas. The foot is held in one hand by the physician and the knuckle of the first interphalangeal joint of the other index finger is

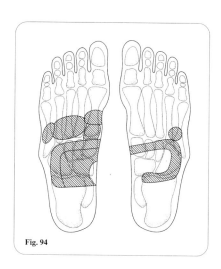

Fig. 94

166

used to apply pressure from toes to heel and from heel to toes, and also to apply massage to above areas 3-4 times (Fig. 94).

(2) Foot acupuncture:

1) Meridianal acupoints: At Taibai (SP 3) and Gongsun (SP 4) acupoints, a reinforcing acupuncture technique is applied for deficient type patients and a reducing technique is applied for excessive type patients. The needles are retained for 20 minutes, or moxibustion is applied for 15 minutes to patients with Yang deficiency or with cold and damp pathogens.

2) Extra acupoints: At Yinyang (EX-F 5) and Nuxi (EX-F 6) acupoints, a reducing technique is applied to excessive type patients and a reinforcing technique is applied to deficient type patients. The needles are retained for 20 minutes, or moxibustion is applied for 15 minutes to patients with cold and damp pathogens or Yang deficiency.

3) Foot acupoints: At Spleen (FA-P 10), Small intestine (FA-P 11) and Colon (FA-P 13) acupoints, a reducing technique is applied to excessive type patients, and a reinforcing technique is applied to deficient type patients. The needles are retained for 20 minutes, or moxibustion is applied for 15 minutes to patients with cold and damp pathogens or Yang deficiency.

(3) External application of drugs:

1) Diarrhea due to damp-heat pathogens: The powder of Zhusha (cinnabar) 3 gm, Pengsha (borax, fried) 1.8 gm, Shexiang (musk) 0.1 gm, Huoxiao (potassium nitrate) 3 gm, Mengshi (chloride-schist, calcined) 1.2 gm, gold sheet 5 pieces, Xionghuang (realgar) 1.8 gm and Bingpian (borneol) 0.9 gm is mixed with boiled water to prepare a paste for application to coeliac plexus 20, stomach 15, small intestine 25 and spleen 34 reflecting areas, twice a day.

2) Diarrhea due to cold pathogens: Baijiezi (white mustard seed) 9 gm, fresh ginger 120 gm and 3 bulbs of garlic with red skin are fried in sesame oil 180 gm and Tongyou (Tung oil) 60 gm with Zhangdan 120 gm gradually added into pot over a low fire to prepare a paste

for application to above areas, twice a day.

3) Diarrhea due to cold and damp pathogens: Fresh Cang'ercao (cocklebur fruit) 2 portions and fresh ginger 1 portion are boiled to prepare a thin glue. After the dregs are removed Huangdan (yellow lead) is added in a proportion of thin glue 500 gm with Huangdan 120 gm to prepare a paste for application to above reflecting areas.

4) Diarrhea due to deficiency of spleen and stomach: Powder of Kufan (calcined alum) 50 gm and wheat flour 20 gm is mixed with a proper amount of vinegar to prepare a thin paste for application to above areas after spreading over the gauze and affixing with adhesive plaster, 3-5 times a day.

(4) Foot bath:

1) A warm decoction of Gegen (kudzuvine root) 50 gm, Baibiandou (white lablab seed) 100 gm and Cheqiancao (plantain) 150 gm at 30 degrees centigrade is used to soak both feet below ankle joint for 30 to 60 minutes, 2-3 times a day to treat diarrhea due to damp-heat pathogens. Laifuzi (radish seed) 20 gm is added for diarrhea due to indigestion, and Fengxianhua (garden balsam) 30 gm or Guizhi (cinnamon twig) 50 gm is added for diarrhea due to spleen deficiency.

2) A hot concentrated decoction of Guizhencao (hairy begger- ticks) 5 pieces prepared in a barrel is used to steam both feet of children repeatedly, 3-4 times at 5 minute intervals after a rest of 2 minutes between treatments for simple diarrhea. For babies between 1-5 years old only the sole is steamed; for children between 5-15, the entire feet may be steamed; and for severe cases the legs above the feet may also be steamed.

6. Poliomyelitis:

The poliomyelitis recognized by modern medicine is an acute epidemic disease caused by the poliomyelitis virus. In traditional Chinese medicine this disease is believed to be caused by an attack of wind, dampness and heat pathogens through the mouth to the lungs and stomach. At the early stage, patients may suffer from fever, cough, red throat, and vomiting and diarrhea, which are the symptoms caused by the attack of pathogens to the lungs and stomach. They may suffer from pain in limbs due to an invasion of pathogens blocking the meridians and disturbing the circulation of qi and blood; and finally, the numbness and paralysis of the limbs may appear to be due to malnutrition of muscles.

Treatment:

(1) Foot massage:

The massage is applied to pituitary gland 4, head 1, cerebellum 3, coeliac plexus 20, lymph nodes (upper body, 39), lymph nodes (abdomen, 40), stomach 15, small intestine 25, liver 18 and gall-bladder 19 reflecting areas. For paralysis of upper body, shoulder 10, scapula 59, elbow joint 60, trapezius muscle 11, neck 53 and thoracic spine 54 reflecting areas may be added; and for paralysis of lower body, hip joint 38, knee 35, waist 55 and sacrum 56 reflecting areas may be added (Fig. 95).

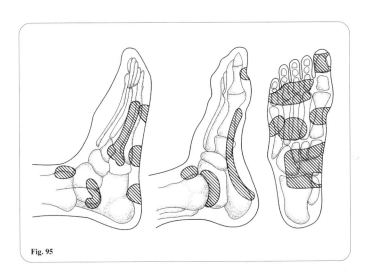

Fig. 95

(2) Foot acupuncture:

1) Meridianal acupoints: At Jiexi (ST 41), Chongyang (ST 42), Neiting (ST 44) and Lidui (ST 45) acupoints, a reducing technique without moxibustion is applied and the needles are retained for 20 minutes.

2) Extra acupoint: A reducing acupuncture technique is applied at Xiakunlun (EX-F 3) and the needle is retained for 20 minutes.

(3) External application of drug:

The powder of Laoyahuateng 60 gm is baked with crystalline sugar, and the hot powder is put into bags for application to the reflecting areas, and changed once every 3 days.

7. Acute convulsions in children:

This is a common acute disease that may include coma, convulsions of limbs, lockjaw, and opisthotonus, usually appearing in children with high fever, meningitis, encephalitis, low blood calcium, cerebral dysgenesis, epilepsy or toxic dysentery.

Treatment:

(1) Foot massage:

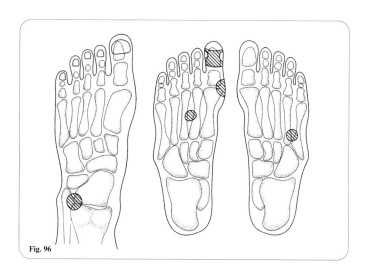

Fig. 96

170

The massage is applied to head 1, adrenal gland 21, pituitary gland 4, parathyroid gland 13, tonsil 45, spleen 34 and lymph nodes (upper body, 39) reflecting areas. The tips of both thumbs are used to apply pressure or the foot is held in one hand by the physician and the knuckle of the first interphalangeal joint of the other index finger is used to massage the reflecting areas 3-5 times (Fig. 96).

(2) Foot acupuncture:

1) Meridianal acupoints: At Yongquan (KI 1), Taichong (LR 3) and Zuqiaoyin (GB 44) acupoints, a reducing acupuncture technique without moxibustion is applied and the needles are retained for 20 minutes.

2) Extra acupoints: At Neizhiyin (EX-F 20) and Lineiting (EX- F 21) acupoints, a reducing technique without moxibustion is applied and the needles are retained for 20 minutes.

(3) External application of drugs:

1) Zhizi (cape-jasmine fruit) powder, Taoren (peach kernel) paste and wheat flour of equal amounts are mixed with 1 egg white to prepare a paste for application on the above reflecting areas to reduce fire and calm the wind.

2) The Xingren (apricot kernel) 7 pieces, Taoren (peach kernel) 7 pieces, Zhizi (cape-jasmine fruit) 7 pieces and fine wheat flour 15 gm are pounded together to prepare a paste for application to adrenal gland 21 and tonsil 45 reflecting areas to clear heart fire and the downward transport qi, resolve blood stasis, tranquilize the mind and calm the wind.

3) Huangqi (milkvetch root) 32 gm, Dangshen (asiabell) 32 gm, Fuzi (aconite lateral root, baked) 32 gm, Baizhu (bighead Atractylodes rhizome), Kouren (nutmeg, roasted) 15 gm, Baishao (white peony root, fried with alcohol) 15 gm, Gancao (licorice, baked with honey) 15 gm, Dingxiang (cloves) 10 gm are fried in sesame oil with Huangdan (yellow lead) to prepare a paste for application with Rougui (cinnamon bark) powder to the above

reflecting areas to warm Zhongjiao (middle energizer) and strengthen spleen.

IV. Surgical and Dermatological Diseases

1. Furuncle and carbuncle:

The furuncle is a common surgical condition usually occuring on the head, face, hand or foot. Mild cases are without serious general symptom, but severe cases may suffer from chills and fever in the early stage, fever, thirst, constipation, dark urine, yellow and greasy tongue coating, and rapid pulse in the middle stage; and the symptoms may gradually disappear with the healing of local lesions in the late stage.

The carbuncle is a pyogenic infection of multiple neighboring hair follicles and sebaceous glands or a confluence of several furuncles, common in aged people or patients with diabetes mellitus. At the early stage, a local dark red and slightly elevated infitrative skin lesion appears with a peripheral hard swelling region but without a clear margin; and at the suppurative stage, many pus plugs appear that may perforate into a form like the mouth of a volcano.

Furuncles and carbuncles have similar etiology, pathogenesis, and symptomatology, and respond to similar therapy, so they are discussed here in combination.

Treatment:

(1) Foot massage:

The massage is applied to reproductive gland 36, lymph nodes (upper body, 39), lymph nodes (abdomen, 40) and adrenal gland 21 reflecting areas (Fig. 97).

(2) Foot acupuncture: Meridianal acupoints: At Zuqiaoyin (GB 44) and Shugu (BL 65) acupoints, a reducing acupuncture technique is applied and the needles are retained for 15 to 20 minutes.

(3) External application of drugs:

Raw Chuanwu (Sichuan aconite root) 3 gm, raw Caowu (wild aconite root) 3 gm, Xixin (wild ginger) 3 gm, Banxia (pinellia tuber) 3 gm and red date without pits 10 pieces are pounded to a paste for preparation of a large pill the size of a dove egg, which is put over Yongquan (KI 1) to treat inflamma tion of the

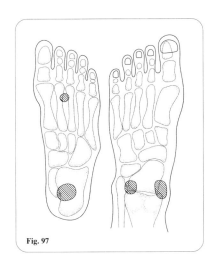

Fig. 97

lymph nodes near the furuncle or carbuncle on the contralateral side of body.

(4) Foot bath:

A warm decoction of Shuizhi (leech) 30 gm, Tubiechong (ground beetle) 10 gm, Taoren (peach kernel) 10 gm, Sumu (sappan wood) 10 gm, Honghua (safflower) 10 gm, Xuejie (dragon's blood) 10 gm, Niuxi (bidentate achyranthes root) 15 gm, Fuzi (aconite lateral root) 15 gm, Guizhi (cinnamon twig) 20 gm, Earthworm 30 gm, Gancao (licorice) 15 gm, Ruxiang (frankincense) 10 gm and Moyao (myrrh) 10 gm in a wooden barrel is used to steam and wash both feet.

2. Acute mastitis:

This is an acute pyogenic infection of the breast during the breast feeding period, more common in primiparae and often in the upper and lateral quarter of one breast.

Treatment:

(1) Foot massage:

The massage is applied to chest 43, lymph nodes (chest, 41), lymph nodes (upper body, 39) and reproductive gland 36 reflecting areas (Fig. 98).

(2) Foot acupuncture:

1) Meridianal acupo-ints: Zulinqi (GB 41), Diwuhui (GB 42), Zhaohai (KI 6), Xiaxi (GB 43), Shugu (BL 65), Xingjian (LR 2) and Taichong (LR 3) acu-points may be selected for application of a reducing acupuncture technique at the early stage of

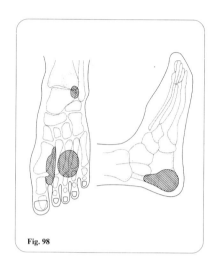

Fig. 98

this disease to promote circulation of qi, release blood stasis, and relieve pain.

2) Foot acupoint: A moderate acupuncture is applied at Lung (FA-P 6) acupoint and the needle is retained for 20 minutes.

3. Hyperplasia of breast:

This is a common disease of middle-aged and older women with breast masses caused by stagnation of liver qi or accumulation of phlegm and dampness.

Treatment:

(1) Foot massage:

The massage is applied to chest 43, lymph nodes (chest, 41), lymph nodes (upper body, 39), lymph nodes (abdomen, 40), kidney 22, ureter 23, urinary bladder 24 and reproductive gland 36 reflecting areas on foot for 20 to 30 minutes. The massage should be applied over a long period of time, and the massage should also be applied thoroughly to the chest at the same time (Fig. 99).

(2) Foot acupuncture:

1) Meridianal acupoints: At Zulinqi (GB 41), Diwu-hui (GB 42) and Taichong (LR 3) acupoints, a reducing or balanced reinforce-reducing acupuncture technique is selected depending on the nature of the disease. The needles are retained for 30 minutes.

2) Foot acupoint: A light stimulation of acupuncture is applied at Lung (FA-P 6) acupoint and the needle is retained for 30 minutes.

4. Erysipelas:

This is an acute contact infectious skin disease displaying a fresh red skin lesion.

Treatment:

(1) Foot massage:

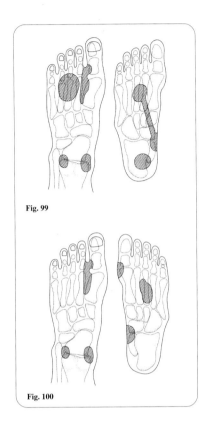

Fig. 99

Fig. 100

Either the parathyroid gland 13, adrenal gland 21, kidney 22 and urinary bladder 24 reflecting areas, or the lymph nodes on upper body and in abdomen or chest 39, 40 or 41 reflecting areas may be selected for massage depending on the location of the skin lesions (Fig. 100).

(2) Foot acupuncture:

Foot acupoint: A strong stimulation is applied at Lung (FA-P 6) acupoint and the needle is retained for 20 minutes.

5. Acute cholecystitis:

This is an acute pyogenic infection of the gallbladder caused by bacterial infection and bile stasis.

Treatment:

(1) Foot massage:

The massage is applied to liver 18, gallbladder 19, stomach 15, duodenum 16 and lymph nodes (upper body, 39) reflecting areas, or kidney 22, ureter 23 and urinary bladder

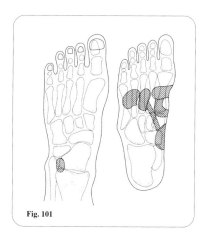

Fig. 101

24 reflecting areas for cholecystitis caused by gallstones (Fig. 101).

(2) Foot acupuncture:

1) Meridianal acupoints: At Zuqiaoyin (GB 44), Diwuhui (GB 42) and Zulinqi (GB 41) acupoints, a reducing acupuncture technique is applied and the needles are retained for 30 to 60 minutes.

2) Extra acupoint: A reducing acupuncture technique is applied at Quchi (EX-F 10) acupoint and the needle is retained for 30 minutes.

3) Foot acupoint: A strong acupuncture stimulation is applied at Liver (FA-P 9) acupoint and the needle is reatained for 20 minutes.

6. Diseases of prostate gland:

Hyperplasia of the prostate gland and prostatitis are two major diseases of this gland. Male patients with hyperplasia of the prostate gland may suffer from dysuria, frequent urination at night, incomplete urination, fine urine streams, and auria and retention of urine accompanied by soreness and pain in waist and weakness of limbs. Dysuria and incomplete urination in middle-aged and older women may also be treated by the following methods.

Treatment:

(1) Foot massage:

The mas sage is applid to prostate gland 50, ureter 51, kidney 22, adrenal gland 21, urethra 23, urinary bladder 24, lymph nodes (abdomen, 40) and sacrum 56 reflecting areas (Fig. 102).

The foot massage is applied for 10 minutes and a good effect can be obtained after a

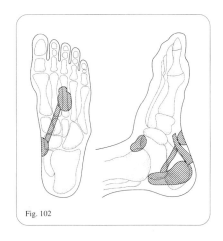

Fig. 102

treatment for 3 days, with a reduction of urination frequency and an increase of urine discharge. At the same time, patients may be fatigued, but this may disappear after the condition is further improved. A burning cigarette can be used to do moxibustion at adrenal gland 21, reproductive gland 36, kidney 22, ureter 23, urinary bladder 24, lumbar spine 55 and sacrum 56 reflecting areas producing an apparent effect.

(2) Foot acupuncture:

1) Meridianal acupoints: At Zhiyin (BL 67), Yongquan (KI 1), Dazhong (KI 4), Shuiquan (KI 5), Zhaohai (KI 6), Dadun (LR 1), Xingjian (LR 2), Taichong (LR 3) and Zhongfeng (LR 4) acupoints, a balanced reinforce-reducing acupuncture technique is applied and the needles are retained for 20 minutes.

2) Extra acupoint: A balanced reinforce-reducing technique is applied at Quchi (EX-F 10) acupoint and the needle is retained for 30 minutes.

3) Foot acupoints: At Spleen (FA-P 10), Kidney (FA-P 14), Urinary bladder (FA-P 15) and Bed-wetting (FA-P 21) acupoints, a moderate

acupuncture stimulation is applied and the needles are retained for 30 minutes.

7. Hemorrhoids:

This is an anal condition with the dilatation and distortion of submucosal venule plexus of lower rectum and subcutaneous venule plexus of anal canal forming venous clamps. Hemorrhoids can be classified as external, internal and mixed types. In traditional Chinese medicine hemorrhoids are believed caused by improper diet with too much uncooked, cold and spicy food, indulgence in alcohol, constipation, and over exertion of bowel movements.

Treatment:

(1) Foot massage:

1) Hemorrhoids: The massage is applied to anus 32, rectum 31. anus and rectum 52, sacrum 56, small intestine 25 and transverse colon 29 reflecting areas.

2) Anal fistula: The massage is applied to anus and rectum 52, adrenal gland 21, urinary bladder 24, lymph nodes (upper body, 39) and lymph nodes (abdomen, 40) reflecting areas (Fig. 103).

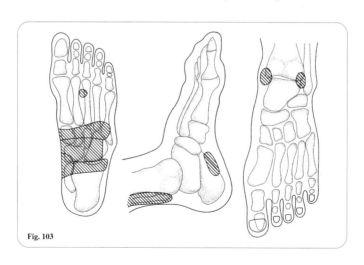

Fig. 103

178

(2) Foot acupuncture:

Meridianal acupoints: At Shangqiu (SP 5), Taichong (LR 3), Xiaxi (GB 43), Gongsun (SP 4), Zhaohai (KI 6), Jinggu (BL 64) and Dazhong (KI 4) acupoints, a reducing acupuncture technique is applied and the needles are retained for 20 minutes. Acupuncture or embedding acopuncture at Shugu (BL 65) may produce a good analgesic effect after an anal operation.

8. Constrictive tenosynovitis:

This is a disease caused by chronic strain of the fingers and wrist related to certain occupations. Forceful or repetitive physical exertion on the job with the fingers and wrist over a long period of time may cause edema, hyperplasia of granulomatous tissue and adhesion of tendon and tendon sheath due to repeated friction, so that the movement of the tendons may be impaired.

A finger lesion is tenosynovitis of flexor muscle of fingers, and a wrist lesion is the constrictive tenosynovitis of the radial styloid process.

Treatment:

Foot massage:

The massage may be applied to the correspondent reflecting areas on foot and the correspondent region of the hand lesion, on the same-side foot. For example, the massage may be applied on the left ankle joint to treat tenosynovitis of the left wrist joint, and the massage is applied to the correspondent joint of the toe to treat the finger joint lesion on the same side.

9. Soft tissue sprain:

This is an injury to soft tissues, including muscles, tendons, ligaments and blood vessels, without bone fracture, dislocation of joint or rupture of the skin and muscles. The patient may suffer from local swelling and pain and limited movement. Before applying foot therapy, bone fracture, joint dislocation, and rupture of ligaments or other bone diseases should be ruled out.

Treatment:

(1) Foot massage:

The reflecting areas are selected according to the location of the injury.

Neck: Neck 7, cervical spine 53, trapezius muscle 14 and coeliac plexus 20 reflecting areas.

Shoulder: Shoulder 10, scapula 59 and hip joint 38 reflecting areas.

Wrist joint: According to the close correlation of hand and foot, the massage is applied to the ankle joint.

Waist: Lumbar spine 55, thoracic spine 54, sacrum 56, sciatic nerve 58, lymph nodes (abdomen, 40), adrenal gland 21 and kidney 22 reflecting areas.

Hip region: Hip joint 38, adrenal gland 21, kidney 22, lumbar spine 55, sacrum 56 and sciatic nerve 58 reflecting areas.

Knee: Knee 35, adrenal gland 21, kidney 22, ureter 23 and urinary bladder 24 reflecting areas (Fig. 104).

The massage is repeatedly applied with the pressure gradually

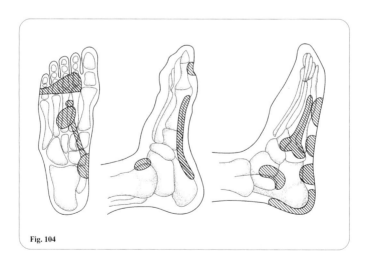

Fig. 104

180

increased, and the patients are asked to gently move their affected region to obtain better results.

(2) Foot acupuncture:

1) Meridianal acupoints: At Kunlun (BL 60), Shugu (BL 65), Diwuhui (GB 42), Shenmai (BL 62), Yongquan (KI 1), Taixi (KI 3), Xingjian (LR 2) and Qiuxu (GB 40) acupoints, a reducing acupuncture technique is applied and the needles are retained for 20 to 30 minutes. Moxibustion may be applied in cases of chronic lesions.

2) Extra acupoints: At Xiakunlun (EX-F 3) and Quanshengzu (EX-F 7) acupoints, a reducing acupuncture technique is applied and the needles are retained for 20 minutes.

3) Foot acupoints: The acupoints are selected according to the location of lesion: Stiff neck (FA-D 6) acupoint is selected for lesion of neck; Lumbago (FA-D 4) and Kidney (FA-P 14) acupoints for lesion of waist; and the Waist and leg (FA-D 9), Ischium 1 (FA-P 18) and Ischium 2 (FA-D 5) acupoints for lumbago. A strong acupuncture stimulation is applied for acute injury, and a moderate stimulation is applied for chronic injury. The needles are retained for 20 minutes.

(3) External application of drug:

The powder of Fuzi (raw aconite lateral root) 30 gm is mixed with liquor to prepare a paste for application to bilateral Yongquan (KI 1) acupoints.

10. Eczema:

This is a common skin disease with symmetrically distributed and multiform skin lesions and local itching. The lesions can be classified as acute, subacute and chronic types.

Treatment;

(1) Foot massage:

The massage is applied to parathyroid gland 13, lung 14, adrenal gland 21, kidney 22, ureter 23, urinary bladder 24, coeliac plexus

20 and spleen 34 reflecting areas and the lymph nodes (upper body, chest and abdomen, 39, 41 and 40) reflecting areas according to the location of skin lesions (Fig. 105).

(2) Foot acupuncture:

1) Meridianal acupoints: A reducing acupuncture technique is applied to Dadu (SP 2) acupoint with the needle retained for 20 minutes to clear heat and resolve dampness.

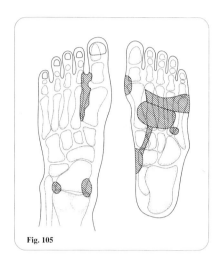
Fig. 105

2) Foot acupoints: A moderate acupuncture stimulation is applied to Lung (FA-P 6) and Tonsil 1 (FA-D 2) acupoints with the needles retained for 20 minutes.

11. Urticaria:

This is an allergic skin disease caused by eating shrimp or crab, administration of drugs or parasite in the body. Symptoms include the sudden appearance of skin lesions all over the body, and even over the mucosa. The lesions may disappear without a trace left on the skin after a few hours. Later, the skin lesions may reappear again, group by group. In chronic patients the skin lesions may relapse in several weeks, months, or even over several years. The skin lesions are slightly bulged papules varying in size from the sesames to beans, or even as large as walnuts, and they may increase in size after scratching. Besides the local burning sensation and severe itching, patients may also suffer from nausea, vomiting, abdominal pain, diarrhea and other digestive tract symptoms if the lesions appear on the mucosa of the stomach and intestines, and severe cases may develop edema of the throat with dyspnea and syncope.

Treatment:

(1) Foot massage:

The massage is applied to lung 14, parathyroid gland 13, kidney 22, transverse colon 29, liver 18, gallbladder 19, adrenal gland 21 and lymph nodes (upper body, chest and abdomen, 39, 41 and 40) reflecting areas (Fig. 106)

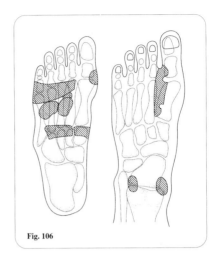

Fig. 106

(2) Foot acupuncture:

1) Meridianal acupoints: A reducing acupuncture technique is applied to Yongquan (KI 1) and Neiting (ST 44) acupoints for acute type, and a balanced reinforce-reducing technique is applied to chronic patients. Moxibustion with ginger at Xingjian (LR 2) and Jiexi (ST 41) as well as Hegu (LI 4) and Yangchi (TE 4) acupoints on the hand can also produce a good therapeutic effect.

2) Foot acupoints: A strong acupuncture stimulation is applied to Lung (FA-P 6) and Ischium (FA-P 18) acupoints for acute type, and a gentle stimulation is applied for chronic patients. The needles are retained for 20 minutes.

12. Alopecia areata:

This is a disease of the scalp with loss of hair in localized areas. The hair may be suddenly lost overnight in a single or multiple areas, varying in size and shapes such as round, elliptic or irregular. Nearby patches may fuse to form a confluent area covered with smooth and shiny skin and surrounded by a well-defined margin. On the bared scalp, the hair follicle holes are clearly visible, but without any sign of inflammation. Patients with alopecia totalis may lose all the hair on the scalp, and patients with alopecia disseminata may also lose their eyebrows, beard and axillary hair in addition to total scalp hair loss.

Treatment:

(1) Foot massage:

The massage is applied to kidney 22, lung 14, head 1, pituitary gland 4, parathyroid gland 13, adrenal gland 21, ureter 23, urinary bladder 24 and reproductive gland 36 reflecting areas (Fig. 107).

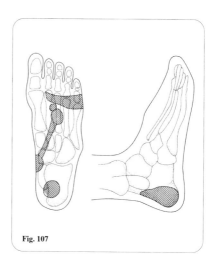

Fig. 107

According to traditional Chinese medicine, the growth of hair is closely related to the kidney and lungs. Therefore, the kidney 22 and lung 14 areas are the first choice for massage treatment and other areas may also be selected according to the condition of the patient. Massage stimulation should be maintained for a longer time than usual for this condition.

(2) Foot acupuncture:

1) Meridianal acupoints: A reinforcing acupuncture technique is applied to Gongsun (SP 4) for tranquilization of the mind and improvement of sleep, and the needle is retained for 30 minutes. Moxi-bustion may be applied at Taixi (KI 3) to reinforce kidney qi and promote hair growth.

2) Foot acupoints: A gentle acupuncture stimulation is applied to

Head and face (FA-P 1), Anmian (FA-P 2), Lung (FA-P 6) and Kidney (FA-P 14) acupoints and the needles are retained for 30 minutes.

V. Diseases of Eye, Ear, Nose, and Throat

1. Red eyes:

This is an acute eye disease with redness, swelling and pain of the eyes, photophobia, watery or dry in eyes and difficulty opening the eyes. Acute conjunctivitis, pseudomembranous conjunctivitis and epidemic keratoconjunctivitis recognized by modern medicine are the same as this disease and can be treated by the following methods.

Treatment:

(1) Foot massage:

The massage is applied to eye 8, frontal sinus 2, head 1, kidney 22, liver 18, lymph nodes (upper body, 39) and lymph nodes (abdomen, 40) reflecting areas (Fig. 108).

(2) Foot acupuncture:

1) Meridianal acupoints: Neiting (ST 44), Zulinqi (GB 41), Diwuhui (GB 42), Xiaxi (GB 43), Zuqiaoyin (GB 44), Kunlun (BL 60), Shenmai (BL 62), Jinggu (BL 64), Shugu (BL 65), Zutonggu (BL 66), Zhiyin (BL 67), Zhaohai (KI 6), Xingjian (LR 2) and Taichong (LR 3) acupoints may be selected to apply a reducing acupuncture technique, and the needles are retained for 20 to 30 minutes.

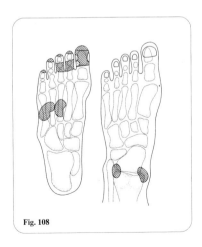

Fig. 108

2) Foot acupoints: A strong acupuncture stimulation is applied at Head and face (FA-P 1), Liver (FA-P 9) and

Kidney (FA-P 14) acupoints and the needles are retained for 20 minutes.

(3) External application of drugs:

1) Red eyes: The powder of Dahuang (raw rhubarb) 15 gm and Tiannanxing (raw Jack-in-the-pulpit tuber) 15 gm is mixed with vinegar to prepare a paste for application to the central area of the soles.

2) Red eyes in children: The powder of Huanglian (Chinese goldthread rhizome) is mixed with water to prepare a paste for application to the central area of the soles.

3) Red eyes in children: The powder of Huhuanglian (Tibet bitter-root) is mixed with tea water to prepare a paste for application to the central area of the palms and soles.

4) Swelling and pain of eyes in children; Dihuang (prepared Rehmannia root) 30 gm is soaked in fresh water and then pounded to prepare a paste for application to the central area of the soles to produce a prompt effect. The paste is affixed by a piece of gauze.

5) Acute and chronic conjunctivitis: The powder of Wuzhuyu (evodia fruit) and Fuzi (prepared aconite lateral root) in equal amounts is mixed with vinegar to prepare a paste for application to both Yongquan (KI 1) acupoints.

6) Ulcer of cornea: The powder of one piece of Tiannanxing (raw Jack-in-the-pulpit tube) and Dahuang (raw rhubarb) in equal amounts is mixed with vinegar to prepare a paste for application to the central area of the soles.

2. Hordeolum (stye):

This is an eye disease with a small itching and painful indurative nodule the size of a grain of wheat on the eyelid.

Treatment:

(1) Foot massage:

The massage is applied to eye 8, parathyroid gland 13, lymph nodes (upper body, 39), lymph nodes (abdomen, 40), kidney 22 and liver 18 reflecting areas (Fig. 109).

(2) Foot acupuncture:

1) At Neiting (ST 44), Zulinqi (GB 41), Diwuhui (GB 42), Xiaxi (GB 43), Zuqiaoyin (GB 44), Shenmai (BL 62), Jinggu (BL 64), Shugu (BL 65), Zhiyin (BL 67), Zhaohai (KI 6), Xingjian (LR 2) and Taichong (LR 3) acupoints, a reducing acupuncture technique is applied and the needles are retained for 20 minutes.

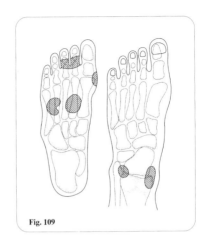

Fig. 109

2) Foot acupoints: At Head and face (FA-P 1), Liver (FA-P 9) and Kidney (FA-P 14) acupoints, a moderate acupuncture stimulation is applied and the needles are retained for 20 minutes.

3. Myopia:

This is an ametropic eye condition in which there is good near sight but poor far sight.

Treatment:

(1) Foot massage:

The massage is applied to eye 8, frontal sinus 2, parathyroid gland 13, kidney 22, adrenal gland 21, ureter 23, urinary bladder 24 and liver 18 reflecting areas (Fig. 110).

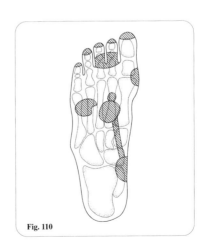

Fig. 110

Because the eye reflecting area on the foot is very small, a probe may be used to apply the massage instead of the finger; but since the reflecting area of liver is much larger, the knuckles of both hands can be used to apply pressure circularly or up and down to increase the stimulation.

(2) Foot acupuncture:

1) Meridianal acupoints: At Neiting (ST 44), Zulinqi (GB 41), Diwuhui (GB 42), Xiaxi (GB 43), Zuqiaoyin (GB 44), Kunlun (BL 60) and Jinggu (BL 64) acupoints, a balanced reinforce-reducing acupuncture technique is applied and the needles are retained for 30 minutes.

2) Foot acupoints: At Head and face (FA-P 1), Liver (FA-P 9) and Kidney (FA-P 14) acupoints, a gentle acupuncture stimulation is applied and the needles are retained for 30 to 40 minutes.

4. Optic atrophy:

Patients may have blurred vision or shadows in front of the eyes in the early stage though their eyes may appear completely normal. Later, vision may become further and further impaired to complete blindness. Optic atrophy, papillitis, thrombosis of retinal artery, pigmentary degeneration of retina, and diseases of ocular fundus recognized by modem medicine may show the above symptoms.

Treatment:

(1) Foot massage:

The massage is applied to eye 8, kidney 22, adrenal gland 21, ureter 23, urinary bladder 24, head

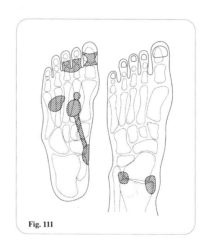

Fig. 111

(brain, 1), brain stem and cerebellum 3, lymph nodes (upper body, 39), lymph nodes (abdomen, 40) and liver 18 reflecting areas for 30 minutes, once or twice a day (Fig. 111).

(2) Foot acupuncture:

1) Meridianal acupoints: At Zulinqi (GB 41), Xingjian (LR 2), Zhaohai (KI 6) and Zhiyin (BL 67) acupoints, a balanced reinforce-reducing acupuncture technique is ap plied and the needles are retained for 30 minutes. Moxibustion may also be applied.

2) Foot acupoints: At Head and face (FA-P 1), Liver (FA-P 9) and Kidney (FA-P 14) acupoints, a moderate acupuncture stimulation is applied and the needles are retained for 20 minutes.

5. Presbyopia:

This is a gradual impairment of vision in people over 50 years of age with normal far vision but blurred near vision. Fatigue of the eyes with heaviness of eyelids, headache, distention of eyes, and blurred vision after reading or writing for a long time can also be treated by foot therapy.

Treatment:

(1) Foot massage:

The massage can be ap plied to eye 8, shoulder 10, neck 7, liver 18, kidney 22 and reproductive gland 36 reflecting areas (Fig. 112). Eye fatigue can be quickly relieved after a basic massage on the sole for 10 minutes, and then a massage on the proximal part of the toes.

(2) Foot acupuncture:

1) Meridianal acupoints:

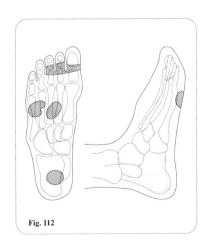

Fig. 112

At Lidui (ST 45), Shugu (BL 65), Zulinqi (GB 41), Diwuhui (GB 42), Zuqiaoyin (GB 44), Shenmai (BL 62), Zhiyin (BL 67), Zhaohai (KI 6), Xingjian (LR 2) and Taichong (LR 3) acupoints, a balanced rein-force-reducing acupuncture technique is applied, the needles are retained for 30 minutes, and sparrow-pecking moxibustion with a burning cigarette can also be applied.

2) Foot acupoints: A gentle acupuncture stimulation can be applied at Head and face (FA-P I), Liver (FA-P 9) and Kidney (FA-P 14) acupoints, the needles are retained for 30 minutes, and moxibustion may also be applied.

6. Nasal bleeding:

This is a nasal condition caused by trauma, inflammation, polyp or tumor of nose, or general diseases of the body including hypertension, arteriosclerosis, hematological diseases, pulmonary cardiac disease, rheumatic fever, intoxication, avitaminosis, and febrile infectious diseases.

Treatment:

(1) Foot massage:

The massage is applied to frontal sinus 2, nose 6, par-athyroid gland 13 and lymph nodes (upper body, chest and abdomen, 39, 41 and 40) reflecting areas (Fig. 113). When the nose bleeds, a gentle massage may be applied to nose 6, parathyroid gland 13 and frontal sinus 2 reflecting areas for 5 to 10 minutes, and at the same time a cold compress applied to

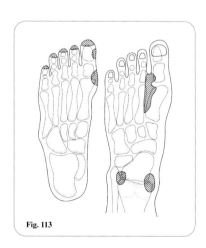

Fig. 113

the forehead and nasal root region also helps stop bleeding.

(2) Foot acupuncture:

1) Meridianal acupoints: At Kunlun (BL 60), Lidui (ST 45), Shenmai (BL 62), Jinggu (BL 64), Zutonggu (BL 66), Zhiyin (BL 67), Yongquan (KI 1), Taixi (KI 3) and Xingjian (LR 2) acupoints, a reducing acupuncture technique is applied and the needles are retained for 30 minutes.

2) Foot acupoints: A moderate acupuncture stimulation is applied at the Head and face (FA-P 1) and Lung (FA-P 6) acupoints and the needles are retained for 20 minutes.

(3) External application of drugs:

1) Nasal bleeding uncontrollable by the oral administration of drugs: Garlic paste the size of a coin, 1-2 mm thick, is applied to the foot contralateral to the nostril reflecting area for nose bleeding and is applied to both feet, if there is bleeding from both nostrils.

2) Nasal bleeding in pregnant women: Wuzhuyu (evodia fruit) 12 gm is soaked in yellow wine for several hours and a wet compress with the tincture is applied to the soles before going to bed; or the powder of Wuzhuyu is mixed with vinegar to prepare a paste for application to the central area of soles.

3) Nasal bleeding: Five bulbs of peeled garlic is pounded with Shengdi (rehmannia root) 15 gm to prepare a paste the size of a coin, 1-2 mm thick, for application at the central area of the sole contralateral to the nostril reflecting area, and at the same time the juice of Jiucaigen (root of Chinese chives) is diluted with water for oral administration. Nasal bleeding will be stopped within 5 minutes.

4) The powder of Dahuang (raw rhubarb), Zhizi (cape-jasmine fruit), Huanglian (Chinese goldthread rhizome), 20 gm each, and Rougui (cinnamon bark) 5 gm, is mixed with vinegar to prepare small cakes for application to Yongquan acupoints to cure nose bleeding caused by heat pathogens in blood.

7. Sinusits:

In addition to a running nose, patients with acute or chronic sinusitis may suffer from distending or pulsating pain in forehead, starting in the morning and reduced in the afternoon, with local tenderness or knocking pain. Patients with acute maxillary sinusitis may suffer from toothache of upper teeth and pain in cheeks with tenderness in notch of the canine tooth. Patients with acute ethmoidal sinusitis may suffer from pain in forehead and inner canthus of eye with tenderness in this region, increase of nasal discharge, nasal obstruction, redness and swelling of nasal mucosa, especially over middle concha, impairment of sense of smell, and purulent discharge in middle meatus of ear.

In recent years, the incidence of allergic rhinitis has increased, and the therapeutic effect of drugs has not been satisfactory. Foot therapy can produce a 90 percent cure rate and 10 percent effective rate. This disease is caused by an allergy to fur, fibers, pollen, dust, and chemicals and patients may suffer from sneezing, running nose, and nasal obstruction.

Treatment:

(1) Foot massage:

1) Sinusitis: The massage is applied to nose 6, parathyroid gland 13, lymph nodes (upper body, 39), lymph nodes (abdomen, 40) and frontal sinus 2 reflecting areas.

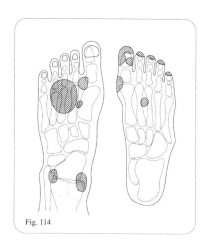

Fig. 114

2) Allergic rhinitis: The massage is applied to nose 6, throat and trachea 48, lung 43, pituitary gland 4, adrenal gland 21 and lymph nodes (upper body,

39) reflecting areas (Fig. 114).

(2) Foot acupuncture:

1) Meridianal acupoint: A reducing acupuncture technique is applied to Jinggu (BL 64) and the needle is retained for 20 minutes.

2) Foot acupoints: A moderate acupuncture stimulation is applied at Head and face (FA-P1) and Lung (FA-P 6) acupoints and the needles are retained for 20 minutes.

(3) External application of drugs:

1) Running nose: A slice of garlic is applied to the central area of soles to produce a good effect.

2) Running nose in aged people: The paste of 4-5 bulbs of single-bulb garlic is applied to the central area of soles and covered with a piece of paper to stop nasal discharge.

3) Nasal obstruction with foul nasal discharge: The powder of Fuzi (raw aconite of lateral root) is mixed with the sticky juice from the hollow tubes of green onion to prepare a paste (35 gm) for application to Yongquan (KI 1) acupoints and covered with a piece of gauze. The paste is changed once a day.

4) Running nose: The powder of Fuzi (raw aconite lateral root) 31 gm, wheat flour 16 gm and green onion 8 gm are pounded with alcohol to prepare a paste for application to the central area of soles.

8. Tinnitus and deafness:

Tinnitus and deafness are conditions affecting the hearing organs. Tinnitus produces a subjective roaring noise in the ears, and deafness is the impairment or total loss of hearing. Tinnitus is often a preliminary symptom of deafness, and they have the similar pathogenesis and respond to similar treatment. Therefore, they are discussed here in combination.

Differential diagnosis:

Excessive type: Tinnitus and deafness of this type are caused by excessive liver and gallbladder fire and a quick onset of accumulation of heat and phlegm. Patients may suffer from deafness, distending and obstructive sensation in ear, and continuous tinnitus like the noise of chirping cicada or tidal roaring, unrelievable by pressing the ear. Patients with excessive liver and gallbladder fire may also have flushed face, dryness in mouth, restlessness, anger, and a wiry pulse.

Deficient type: Tinnitus and deafness of this type are caused by deficient kidney essence for nourishing the ears in chronic patients. They may suffer from interrupted tinnitus of low pitch and mild tone, worse when fatigued, reduced by pressing the ear, and accompanied by dizziness, soreness of waist, emission of semen, leukorrhagia, and feeble and thready pulse.

Hysterical deafness: This is sudden bilateral deafness without tinnitus, dizziness or disturbance of balance function. Patients may have other symptoms of hysteria caused by mental trauma.

These patients may perform self-massage by covering the external ear meatuses with both palms and knocking the occipital region of head with the fingers, and then repeatedly moving the palms away from and back to the meatuses for several minutes, and do the massage every morning and evening.

Treatment:

(1) Foot massage:

The massage is applied to ear 9, labyrinth 42, head 1, lymph nodes (upper body, 39), lymph nodes (abdomen, 40) and parathyroid gland 13 reflecting areas (Fig. 115).

(2) Foot acupuncture:

1) Meridianal acupoints: At Neiting (ST 44), Zulinqi (GB 41), Diwuhui (GB 42),

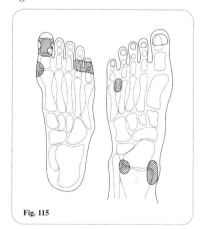

Fig. 115

194

Xiaxi (GB 43), Zuqiaoyin (GB 44), Shenmai (BL 62), Jinmen (BL 63), Shugu (BL 65) and Taixi (KI 3) acupoints, a reinforcing acupuncture technique is applied for the deficient type, and a reducing technique is applied for the excessive type. The needles are retained for 20 to 30 minutes.

2) Foot acupoints: At Head and face (FA-P 1), Kidney (FA-P 14) and Vertigo (FA-M 1) acupoints, a gentle stimulation is applied for the deficient type, and a strong stimulation is applied for the excessive type. The needles are retained for 20 minutes.

9. Sudden aphonia:

This is a sudden loss or hoarseness of voice due to acute throat diseases such as sore throat, strained vocal cords, and hysteria recognized by modern medicine.

Treatment:

(1) Foot massage:

The massage is applied to throat, trachea and vocal cord 48, tonsil 45, lymph nodes (upper body, 39), lymph nodes (abdomen, 40) and neck 7 reflecting areas (Fig, 116).

(2) Foot acupuncture:

1) Meridianal acupoints: At Yongquan (KI 1), Xingjian (LR 2) and Taixi (KI 3) acupoints, a reducing acupuncture technique is applied and the needles are retained for 20 minutes.

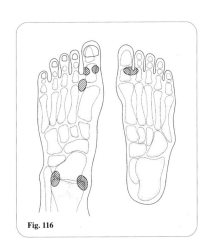

Fig. 116

2) Foot acupoints: At Head and face (FA-P 1), Heart (FA-P 5) and Lung (FA-P 6) acupoints, a strong acupuncture stimulation is

applied and the needles are retained for 20 minutes.

10. Aphtha:

This is a disease of the oral cavity with yellowish white ulcers the size of a pea on the buccal mucosa; and it can be divided into the excessive and deficient types.

Differential diagnosis:

Excessive type: Ulcers are caused by overeating greasy food and indulging in alcohol, accumulation of heat in spleen and stomach and transformation of heat pathogens to fire attacking the oral cavity along the meridian. Ulcers may come and go quickly. Some are yellowish white ulcers on lips, tongue and buccal mucosa in a round or elliptic shape, the size of a pea or soybean, surrounded by a fresh red border. Patients may suffer from local pain, fever, thirst, dark urine, and rapid pulse.

Deficient type: These ulcers are caused by the upward flaming of deficient fire and they are difficult to cure, often with repeated relapses over a long period of time. In general, there are only three kinds of ulcers affecting the oral cavity, yellowish white in color and surrounded by a pink border. The tongue is fresh red in color without coating, and the pulse is feeble and thready.

Treatment:

(1) Foot massage:

The massage is applied to palate 47, lower jaw 46, lymph nodes (upper body, 39), frontal sinus 2 and trigeminal nerve 5 reflecting areas (Fig. 117).

(2) Foot acupuncture:

1) Meridianal acupoint: A

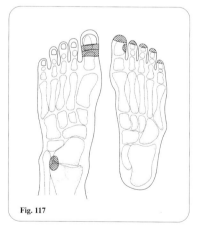

Fig. 117

reducing acupuncture technique is applied to Lidui (ST 45) acupoint, and the needle is retained for 10 minutes, and bleeding therapy with a three-edged needle may also be applied.

2) Foot acupoints: At Head and face (FA-P 1), Heart (FA-P 5) and Kidney (FA-P 14) acupoints, a moderate acupuncture stimulation is applied and the needles are retained for 30 minutes.

(3) External application of drugs:

1) The powder of Tiannanxing (raw Jack-in-the-pulpit) 5 gm and Dahuang (raw rhubarb) 5 gm is mixed with vinegar for application to the central area of the soles.

2) Relapsing aphthosis: An equal amount of Fuzi (prepared aconite lateral root) and Rougui (cinnamon bark) is pounded and mixed with vinegar for application to both Yongquan (KI 1) acupoints.

3) Ulceration of mouth and tongue: Earthworm, Wuzhuyu (evodia root) and wheat flour are pounded together to prepare a paste for application to the central area of both soles.

4) The powder of Tiannanxing (raw Jack-in-the-pulpit) tuber 3-5 gm is mixed with vinegar to prepare a paste for application to both Yongquan (KI 1) acupoints overnight for several days. Because of the poisonous property of this paste, it is prohibited for oral administration.

5) Ulceration of oral cavity in children: The powder of Wuzhuyu (evodia fruit) is mixed with one egg white to prepare small pills the size of a broad bean for application on both Yongquan (KI 1) acupoints and fixed with adhesive plaster, once every other day, 2-3 times.

6) Ulcers in oral cavity of newborn babies with difficulty sucking milk: The powder of alum is mixed with one egg white to prepare a paste for application to both Yongquan (KI 1) acupoints, changed after it dries.

11. Toothache:

There are five types of this common symptom of disease in the oral cavity.

Differential diagnosis:

Toothache due to caries: Tooth pain may come and go from time to time, and may be induced by chewing food with the bad tooth.

Toothache caused by wind and heat pathogens: Besides the toothache relievable by cold, patients may also have swelling of gums, difficulty chewing food, swelling and redness of cheek, thirst, red tip of tongue with white and dry coating, and floating and rapid pulse.

Toothache caused by wind and cold pathogens: Patients may suffer from toothache relievable by heat, chills induced by blowing wind, no thirst, white and slippery tongue coating, and slow and moderate pulse.

Toothache due to heat pathogens in stomach: Patients may suffer from toothache, swelling of gums, thirst, foul odor from mouth, constipation, yellow and dry tongue coating, and full and rapid pulse.

Toothache due to deficient fire pathogens: A dull toothache may come and go from time to time, with loosened tooth root, flushed cheeks, dryness in throat, red tongue tip, and thready and rapid pulse.

Treatment:

(1) Foot massage:

The massage is applied to neck 7, palate 47, low jaw 46, stomach 15, liver 18, small intestine 25 and lymph nodes (upper body, 39) reflecting areas (Fig. 118).

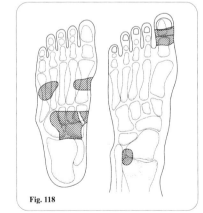

Fig. 118

(2) Foot acupuncture:

1) Meridianal acupoints: At Chongyang (ST 42),

Neiting (ST 44), Lidui (ST 45), Zulinqi (GB 41), Kunlun (BL 60) and Taixi (KI 3) acupoints, a balanced reinforce- reducing acupuncture technique is applied for toothache due to defi cient fire pathogens, and a reduc ing acupuncture technique is ap plied for other types of toothache. The needles are retained for 30 minutes.

2) Extra acupoints: A reduc ing acupuncture technique is applied to Waihuaiqian Jiaomai (EX-F 1), Nuxi (FA-F 6) and Bafeng (FA-F 22) acupoints and the needles are retained for 20 minutes.

3) Foot acupoints: A strong acupuncture stimulation is applied at Head and face (FA-P 1), Toothache 1 and 2 (FA-P 19 and 20) acupoints and the needles are retained for 30 minutes. Kidney (FA-P 14) acupoint is added for toothache due to deficient fire pathogens.

(3) External application of drugs:

1) Toothache due to Yin deficiency: The powder of Fuzi (raw aconite lateral root) is mixed with water to prepare a paste for application to the central area of both soles.

2) Toothache due to kidney deficiency: The powder of Fuzi (aconite lateral root) 15 gm, Wuzhuyu (evodia fruit) 15 gm, Xixin (wild ginger) 15 gm, and Dahuang (rhubarb) 6 gm is mixed with vinegar to prepare a paste for application to Yongquan (KI 1) acupoints. The paste is changed once a day.

3) Suppuration of tooth root: The powder of Dahuang (raw rhubarb) 9 gm, Dingxiang (cloves) 10 grains and mung bean 6 gm is mixed with vinegar to prepare a paste for application to the central area of the soles.

12. Sore throat:

A sore throat can be caused by external pathogens or internal injury. Differential diagnosis:

Sore throat caused by external pathogens: The onset is prompt and the clinical course is short. At the early stage the patient may have symptoms caused by external pathogens, including fever, chills induced by blowing wind, headache, and cough. Then the patient may develop dryness, a burning sensation, slight redness, and swelling and pain in throat with mild dysphagia. Following the development of the disease, the pain, redness and swelling in throat become more and more severe, together with a blocking sensation of a foreign body, spitting of yellow and sticky sputum, hoarseness of voice, and difficulty speaking. The pulse is floating and rapid.

Sore throat caused by internal injury: The onset is insidious and the clinical course is longer. Symptoms such as swelling and dryness and pain in throat can be aggravated by fatigue, but local redness and swelling is not as marked as that in patients whose condition is caused by external pathogens. At the early stage, the throat is slightly red and swollen with mild pain when eating. But severe cases may include ulceration of throat with white purulent spots. The symptoms are mild in the morning, worse in the afternoon, and much more severe at night. Patients may also suffer from dryness in throat and tongue, flushed cheek and lips, hotness in palms and soles, mental fatigue, fresh red tongue, and thready and rapid pulse.

Treatment:

(1) Foot massage:

The massage is applied to neck 7, tonsil 45, throat 48, ear 9, chest 43, lymph nodes (upper body, 39), kidney 22, adrenal gland 21 and urinary bladder 24 reflecting areas (Fig 119).

The knuckles of index and middle fingers are used to knead and rub ear 9 reflecting area to lateral side and to massage neck 7 reflecting area. The thumb is used to carefully massage kidney 22 reflecting area. A probe is used to gently and slowly apply massage on lymph nodes (upper body, 39) reflecting area, because it is small and sensitive.

(2) Foot acupuncture:

1) Meridianal acupoints: For sore throat caused by external pathogens, a reducing acupuncture technique is applied at Neiting (ST 44), Chongyang (ST 42), Lidui (ST 45) and Zulinqi (GB 41) acupoints. For sore throat caused by internal injury, a reinforcing acupuncture technique is applied at Yongquan (KI 1), Taixi (KI 3),

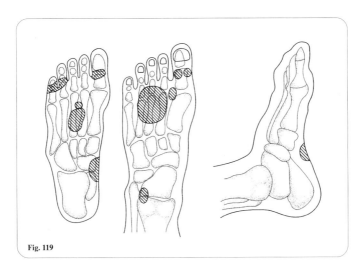

Fig. 119

Zhaohai (KI 6) and Taichong (LR 3) acupoints and the needles are retained for 20 minutes. Bleeding therapy at Lidui (ST 45) with a three-edged needle, and finger-pressing massage at Rangu (KI 2) can also be used to treat sore throat.

2) Foot acupoints: At Tonsil 1 and 2 (FA-D 2 and 3), Head and face (FA-P 1) and Heart (FA-P 5) acupoints, a strong acupuncture stimulation is applied for the excessive type, and a moderate stimulation is also applied to Kidney (FA-P 14) acupoint for the deficient type. The needles are retained for 20 minutes.

(3) External application of drugs:

1) The powder of Fuzi (prepared aconite lateral root) 15 gm, Wuzhuyu (evodia fruit) 15 gm, Xixin (wild ginger) 15 gm and Dahuang (rhubarb) 6 gm is mixed with vinegar to prepare small cakes for application to Yongquan (KI 1) acupoints, once a day, to treat sore throat caused by kidney deficiency and the upward flaming of deficient fire.

2) The powder of hot pepper and wheat flour are mixed with water to prepare a paste for application of wet compress to both soles for

2-3 hours.

3) A fine powder of Fuzi (raw aconite lateral root) or Wuzhuyu (evodia root) is mixed with hot vinegar for application to the central area of both soles.

(4) Foot bath:

The feet are soaked in hot salt water to relieving the symptoms of sore throat.

图书在版编目（CIP）数据

足疗治百病：英文／纪青山编著.

北京：外文出版社，2009（中国传统养身保健）

ISBN 978-7-119-05998-3

I. 足… II. 纪… III. 足－按摩疗法（中医）－英文 IV. R244.1

中国版本图书馆CIP数据核字（2009）第152250号

责任编辑：孙海玉　杨　璐　刘芳念

图片绘制：姚亚妮　罗　剑　等

内文设计：北京维诺传媒文化有限公司

封面设计：一瓢设计

印刷监制：张国祥

足疗治百病

纪青山　李　杰　编著

王　台　英译

© 2009　外文出版社

出 版 人：呼宝民

总 编 辑：李振国

出版发行：外文出版社

　中国北京百万庄大街24号

　邮政编码 100037

　http://www.flp.com.cn

印　　刷：北京外文印刷厂

开本：710×1010　1/16 印张：13.75

2009年第2版 第2次印刷

　（英）

ISBN 978-7-119-05998-3

07500（平）